This book was produced by and all royalties from it will go to the **American Society of Marine Artists**.

See the expanded edition of this book with over 90 full color illustrations. Also available for kindle.

Artists whose work appears in this book are members of the American Society of Marine Artists, the nation's oldest and largest not-for-profit, educational, professional organization dedicated to the promotion and understanding of marine art and history. This 501.C.3 association seeks to encourage the free exchange of ideas among artists. Its members come from across the United States, Canada and abroad and are artists, galleries, organizations and individuals interested in marine art and history. If you share these interests, come aboard. Visit the Society's web site to learn more about how to become a member.

www.americansocietyofmarineartists.com

The American Society of Marine Artists
also produced the video documentary series upon which this book is based. It can be found at this link and is free to all:
www.naval-war-of-1812-illustrated.org

The Naval War of 1812-1815

Foundation of America's Maritime Might

Written by

Charles Raskob Robinson

With Glossary Of Nautical Terms Used In This Book

Printed in the United States of America

First printing, 2015

ISBN-13: 978-0692370339 (American Society of Marine Artists)

ISBN-10: 0692370331

Published by the American Society of Marine Artists
1410 South 18th Street
Saint Louis, MO 63104

The nation's oldest and largest professional not-for-profit educational organization dedicated to marine art and history.
Society's web site: www.americansocietyofmarineartists.com
Video documentary: www.naval-war-of-1812-illustrated.org

NAVAL WAR OF 1812 - 1815

TABLE OF CONTENTS

ILLUSTRATION CREDITS

i. FOREWORD

1. CHAPTER ONE *The Why, What and Who*

9. CHAPTER TWO *Prologue to War: The Causes of the War and the Development of the United States Maritime Forces*

25. CHAPTER THREE *War on Blue Water, Part I: Early American Naval Victories*

39. CHAPTER FOUR *War on Blue Water, Part II: The British Blockade of American Ports and Economic Lockdown*

61. CHAPTER FIVE *War on the Lakes*

85. CHAPTER SIX *War on Brown Water*

109. CHAPTER SEVEN *Epilogue*

119. GLOSSARY OF NAUTICAL TERMS

131. ACKNOWLEDGMENTS

NAVAL WAR OF 1812 - 1815

ILLUSTRATION CREDITS

COVER: ***U.S. Frigate Constitution*** Meets the ***H.M. Frigate Guerriere*** by Robert Sticker (1922 – 2011), Fellow of the American Society of Marine Artists; front and back cover design by Michael James Killelea, Signature Member of the American Society of Marine Artists

TABLE OF CONTENTS: Gun Deck Aft by Robert Sticker (1922 – 2011), Fellow of the American Society of Marine Artists

ILLUSTRATION CREDITS: ***U.S. Frigate United States*** by Geoffrey Hunt, Member of the American Society of Marine Artists and Member and Past President of the Royal Society of Marine Artists

NAVAL WAR OF 1812 -1815

FOREWORD: ***U.S. Frigate Constitution*** in Sicily by Christopher Travers Blossom, Fellow and Past President of the American Society of Marine Artists.

CHAPTER ONE: ***U.S. Frigate Constitution*** at Sea by John Stobart, Fellow Emeritus of the American Society of Marine Artists

CHAPTER TWO: New York Harbor in 1790 by Lewis Victor Mays, Fellow Emeritus of the American Society of Marine Artists

CHAPTER THREE: ***U.S. Sloop-of-War Hornet*** vs. ***H.M. Brig Peacock***: After the Action, Claiming the Prize by Mark Myers, Fellow Emeritus of the American Society of Marine Artists and Member and Past President of the Royal Society of Marine Artists

CHAPTER FOUR: ***H.M.S. Ramillies*** off Block Island, 1813 by Lewis Victor Mays, Fellow Emeritus of the American Society of Marine Artists

CHAPTER FIVE: Battle of Lake Erie by Patrick Lyons O'Brien, Signature Member of the American Society of Marine Artists

CHAPTER SIX: Fort McHenry by Mark Myers, Fellow Emeritus of the American Society of Marine Artists and Member and Past President of the Royal Society of Marine Artists

CHAPTER SEVEN: ***U.S.S. Harry S. Truman***: Instrument of Foreign Policy in the Persian Gulf by James Riley Griffiths, Signature Member of the American Society of Marine Artists

GLOSSARY OF NAUTICAL TERMS USED IN THIS BOOK: The Second Salvo by Robert Sticker (1922 – 2011), Fellow of the American Society of Marine Artists

ACKNOWLEDGMENTS: ***H.M. Frigate Shannon*** vs. ***U.S. Frigate Chesapeake*** by Peter Rindlisbacher, Ph.D., Member of the American Society of Marine Artists and an Artist Member of the Canadian Society of Marine Artists

NAVAL WAR OF 1812 -1815

FOREWORD

By William S. Dudley, Ph.D.
Former Director of Naval History for the United States Navy

During the recent nearly three-year Bicentennial of the War of 1812, the American public has been treated to a national cultural event. This is seen in a significant outpouring of monographs and popular histories, symposia, seminars, museum exhibits, conferences, and television programs on the war. They dwelt on its misunderstood origins, tortuous developments, economic and political ramifications and, for both Americans and Canadians, a fortunate though not foregone termination. Among these notable offerings was the American Society of Marine Artists' production of The Naval War of 1812 Illustrated.

In the United States, historians, tourism specialists, and film producers anticipated the bicentennial opportunities by setting to work in their research several years in advance. It was my good fortune to have been present when Charles Raskob Robinson of the American Society of Marine Artists attended a meeting of the Maritime Committee at the Maryland Historical Society in 2009. At that time he raised the subject of a traveling art exhibit based on the War of 1812. We discussed the practical difficulties and expense of doing this, particularly at a time when most Chesapeake museums would want to retain their marine art for display during the bicentennial. The "aha" moment came when a younger member of the group asked if we had considered creating an on-line exhibit of these paintings which would be much more efficient and less costly to create. This gave birth to an idea that Robinson dwelled upon and then used to create what has become the premier on-line art exhibition/ video documentary of the bicentennial, called the Naval War of 1812 Illustrated. From this project came the idea of writing a book based on the video documentary. Charlie was kind enough to offer me an opportunity to write the book's Foreword.

* * *

Since 1789, the year of the French Revolution, the monarchs of Europe had worried about the spread of republicanism, particularly after the imprisonment of King Louis XVI and his Austrian Queen Marie Antoinette in early 1792. Austria had threatened war with France should any harm come to its rulers. To pre-empt this, France declared war against Austria and its ally, Prussia. After the execution of the French king and queen in 1793, the Austrian, Prussian, and British monarchies formed a coalition to suppress the French contagion before it could spread abroad. In response, the French Republic called up and trained a large citizen army to contend with the coalition.

This was the beginning of more than twenty years of nearly continuous warfare across Europe. With the rise of General Napoleon Bonaparte as First Consul of France in 1799, the Wars of the French Revolution became known as the Napoleonic Wars and spread their tentacles across the oceans and around the world to wherever Britain and France had colonies. This deadly conflict restricted the trade of neutral nations like the United States. At the same time, ships of the Royal Navy had been halting American merchant ships and impressing their seamen since the beginning of their war with France in the 1790s. As a form of economic reprisal, the United States in 1807 prohibited trade with both Britain and France, the result of which impoverished American merchants engaging in sea trade and provoked others into smuggling across the border with Canada. While this move had no immediate impact on the maritime war, it did represent a final American effort to bring about a change in British policy short of war. Eventually, British warships discovered French warships and privateers refitting in Chesapeake waters. This led to clashes such as the *Chesapeake-Leopard* and *President-Little Belt* affairs, which created hostility and expectation of war between the U. S. Navy and the Royal Navy. The issues of impressment of seamen and confiscation of American merchant ships by Britain and France provoked anger and a thirst for retaliation, and became primary causes of the War of 1812.

Lingering antagonism between American settlers and Native American tribes in the Old Northwest (Ohio, Indiana, and Michigan) led to the outbreak of warfare at the Battle of Tippecanoe. Animosities reminiscent of the Revolutionary War thirty years earlier compelled some southern and western leaders to call for a second war against Great Britain, and land hunger among others provided support for this cause. When diplomatic efforts and economic sanctions failed, President James Madison and the U.S. Congress declared war against Great Britain on June 18, 1812. Congress, having long anticipated the possibility of war with Britain, was nonetheless ambivalent about funding its requirements. The navalists among President Madison's

Republican majority had been insufficiently strong to pass legislation to authorize the building of new ships and could only wring a concession to repair and rearm those still in commission.

President Madison and his Navy Secretary Paul Hamilton had to go to war with a navy of only sixteen vessels - a handful of frigates, brigs, schooners, and an excessive number of gunboats capable only of harbor defense and coastal embargo enforcement. Arrayed against this tiny naval force was Britain's immense Royal Navy, accustomed to dominating the seas against its ancient foes France and Spain. In 1812, the British navy still had worldwide responsibilities of pursuing, capturing, or blockading the French Navy ships and those of its allies in the Napoleonic Wars. Having been in this fight for over twenty years, the British had plenty of experience in knowing what was required of them. They had on hand ninety-seven ships-of-the-line as opposed to none for the United States, 105 frigates as compared with nine American frigates, and 313 other vessels, a mixture sloops-of-war (ship-sloops), brigs, schooners, and sloops which vastly outnumbered the U.S. Navy.

The military strategy developed by the Madison administration for conducting the War of 1812 involved three small American armies attacking Canada simultaneously during the summer of 1812. Its goal was to capture and hold Canada hostage to gain a reversal of British policies. The U.S. Navy's role in this was to protect American shipping and to attack British commerce on the Atlantic. Virtually no forethought had been given to naval warfare on the Great Lakes in support of the invading armies, or on Chesapeake Bay, should the British choose to operate in American coastal waters. As it happened, after the Royal Navy established the blockade, the inhabitants of the coastal New England and the Chesapeake shores of Virginia and Maryland suffered exceedingly from the dominance of the Royal Navy's presence and the lack of adequate support from the U.S. Navy.

The American government suffered from an excess of optimism in the war's early stages, believing that an invasion of

Canada could be accomplished easily while Britain's attention was focused on supplying its armies in Spain, blockading the coast of France, and protecting the British Isles from invasion. Had Madison and Congress acted a year earlier this might have been true. But in fact, by the time Madison won re-election in November 1812, Napoleon's armies were already in retreat from Russia, and the British Army under General Arthur Wellesley was gaining ground against the French in Spain. As it happened, well-led British regulars backed by an aroused Canadian militia gave stout resistance to the American armies that invaded in summer of 1812. The only good news for Americans came from the high seas where the few strong frigates and sloops-of-war fought skillfully against the ships Britain had allocated for North American waters. Privateers flocked to the cause motivated by patriotism and the purse to take British merchantmen wherever they could be found. During the first eight months of the war, the U.S. Navy defeated four British frigates and two-sloops-of-war in single ship engagements.

Heartened by the naval victories and despite military setbacks, the American voters gave Madison and the Democratic-Republican Party a vote of confidence in the November 1812 elections. Reinforced by popular backing, Madison asked for the resignations of Secretaries of War William Eustis and Navy Paul Hamilton, replacing them with John Armstrong and William Jones, respectively. Congress reacted favorably to his requests for more troops and to authorize the building of additional ships for the Navy. Yet, even as these steps were taken to strengthen the war effort in Washington, there were signs of more difficulties to come. The British Admiralty, disappointed and embarrassed by the defeat of their frigates at the hands of the upstart U.S. Navy, ordered its frigates to avoid single-ship combat battle with the U.S. heavy frigates and extended its commercial and naval blockade of the American coast from New England to the Chesapeake Capes and farther south.

With the defeat of American armies in their first attempt in Canada came U.S. determination to renew the effort in 1813.

Those, whether British or American, who understood the requirements of fighting on the Canadian borderlands urged that naval squadrons be built to fight in coordination with and in support of their armies in the Old Northwest, on the Niagara Peninsula (Ontario), and at Sackets Harbor, New York, on Lake Ontario. For Navy Secretary William Jones, this meant he would have to direct a two-front naval war with limited resources. The British already had a small number of ships on the lakes called the Provincial Marine, though it was under the control of the British Army not the Royal Navy. Against this, the U.S. Navy had but one vessel, ***U.S. Brig Oneida***, based at Sackets Harbor, where its mission was to enforce the embargo. When it became clear that the war would require a considerable naval force in northern waters, Secretary Hamilton ordered Captain Isaac Chauncey to be in command at Sackets Harbor to gain naval control of Lakes Ontario and Erie. Chauncey built a large squadron of frigates, sloops-of-war and converted commercial schooners for Lake Ontario and appointed Master Commandant Oliver Hazard Perry to take charge of building a squadron on Lake Erie. By dint of much hard work and expense, Chauncey was able to create a sufficiently strong force to counter the Royal Navy's new establishment on Lake Ontario but did not force a major battle with his cautious opponent Captain Sir James Lucas Yeo. Perry, in an even more remote post at Erie, Pennsylvania, built a capable squadron centered on two heavy brigs and a dozen converted schooners and defeated Captain Robert Barclay's smaller force on Lake Erie in September 1813. This enabled Perry to carry General William Henry Harrison's army to the north shore of the lake in pursuit of a British Army and its Indian allies under the Shawnee chief Tecumseh, defeating them at the Battle of the Thames. These conditions reduced the threat from Canadian forces for the remainder of the season on the Niagara peninsula. Then, in what was a wasteful and humiliating experience, the Americans sent a small, ill-equipped army under Major General James Wilkinson in several hundred boats down the St. Lawrence River in hopes of taking Montreal and Quebec. This force disembarked on the left bank to engage a pursuing British-Canadian force at Crysler's Farm yet failed to win the day owing to poor leadership. Just two weeks before, a second American army under the command of General Wade Hampton marching north to join forces with Wilkinson had met a similar fate in confronting British regulars and militia from Lower Canada on the banks of Chateauguay River thus ending any threat posed against Montreal and Quebec in the second year of the war. These military failures led to overdue reorganization and new leadership for the U.S. Army in 1814.

In one of the more bizarre, unplanned exploits of the war at sea, in February 1813, Captain David Porter of the ***U.S. Frigate Essex*** took advantage of discretionary orders and sailed his ship westward around Cape Horn and into the eastern Pacific where he pursued and found an undefended British whaling fleet. There, with unfettered abandon, he captured, or burned and sank many whalers over a period of several months. Knowing that sooner or later the Royal Navy would pursue him, he sought refuge in the Marquesas Islands to rest his crew and refit his ship, which had been at sea for over a year. Early in 1814, he sailed for Valparaiso, Chile where he met two British warships sent after him. He might have avoided the confrontation but like others of his generation, he had a strong sense of duty and honor compelling him to meet the enemy. In the battle that followed, in March 1814, the ***H.M. Frigate Phoebe*** and ***Sloop-of-War Cherub*** out-gunned ***Essex,*** which was equipped with only short-range carronades. They destroyed his ship and many of his men, but after capture he and the survivors were given their parole and allowed to sail for home.

Napoleon's defeat became a certainty in late 1813. With his army in ruins and the Allied armies surrounding Paris, the Emperor was forced into exile on the island of Elba. As these events occurred, British reinforcements were on their way to North America. Several brigades of Wellington's army arrived in Canada as more ships-of-the-line and frigates arrived off the American coast in early 1814. Most of the U.S. Navy's ships were blockaded or delayed in sailing until bad weather permitted their escape to sea. Privateers, which in earlier years had sailed easily from Baltimore, New York or Boston, now had to be more circumspect. Hard times had come for landsmen as well. British troops occupied the coast of Maine from Machias to Castine, warships bombarded Stonington, Connecticut and enemy boats raided and burned privateers at Pettipaug (Essex), Connecticut. British raids laid waste to plantations and towns on Chesapeake Bay, burned Washington's public buildings and laid Alexandria under contribution. The nation's finances were undone for lack of tax revenue on imports and exports because the blockaders had virtually halted overseas and coastal trade. The future looked very bleak. And yet, change was in the air.

In July 1814, a new generation of younger generals led an American army to stand up to British regulars at Chippewa, Lundy's Lane, and Fort Erie. General Alexander Macomb fortified and defended Plattsburg, New York, while Master Commandant Thomas Macdonough led his small squadron to victory over a Royal Navy squadron in the Battle of Lake Champlain in September. At virtually the same time, the Major General Samuel Smith and Commodore John Rodgers led Army Soldiers, citizens, and Navy Sailors in the successful defense of Baltimore, repelling a major British invasion force bent on destroying the city. American negotiators had held firm in dialog with their British counterparts in peace negotiations in Ghent, Belgium. When news of the unexpected American victories reached Europe in late October, the diplomatic atmosphere turned in favor of the United States.

The abdication of Napoleon signaled the end of the wars that turned Europe upside down. The governments of Britain, Russia, Austria, Prussia and the court of Louis XVIII of France wanted a secure peace but in order for a return of stability, each wanted to redraw the borders of their kingdoms. They agreed on convoking an international conference in Vienna to decide how Europe was to be governed for the future. The former allies were jockeying for positions of influence. In order for the British to play an important role at the Congress of Vienna, their government had to show that its house was in order and that its military and navy retained the capabilities to support its positions. Yet their setbacks and defeats of recent months in North America weighed heavily on the minds of Britain's statesmen and ambassadors at London, Ghent, and Vienna. Then, too, the human and financial costs of twenty years of warfare were an accumulated heavy burden on Parliament. Finally, it was more important for the British to finish their involvement in an expensive war in North America by yielding on important issues to obtain a peace treaty. Then they could focus their full attention on the Congress of Vienna. Thus, the Treaty of Ghent was signed on December 24, 1814, even as the British were launching an amphibious attack on New Orleans. The British plans for this new raid had been laid many months before the Battles of Plattsburg and Baltimore. The Navy at New Orleans, led by Master Commandant Daniel Patterson, lent vital assistance to General Andrew Jackson, using its gunboats on Lake Borgne and two heavily armed ships on the Mississippi to delay and bedevil the enemy. The final United States' victory at New Orleans on January 8, 1815 ended the land war with a finality that could not be mistaken in Europe and the United States. The fighting at sea continued because of slow communications, but with the exchange of treaty ratifications completed in mid-February, the news of the war's end became official.

* * *

The Naval War of 1812 Illustrated, which masterfully combined art and historic interpretation, has engaged all who were aware of it. This is in my opinion, the best and most balanced video history to have been produced during the bicentennial. The British and Canadian viewpoint is fairly presented, as it should be, to represent the facts and to gain respect from a knowledgeable international audience. Obviously, the focus is naval, though related land warfare is intelligently discussed and the voice-over script is well researched and confidently delivered. A musical soundtrack of original composition based on melodies and ballads of the War of 1812 era in Britain and America makes for pleasant and appropriate listening throughout. It is clear much thought went into the division of this topic into component parts, Introduction, Prologue, Blue Water I, Blue Water II, The Lakes, Brown Waters, and Epilogue. All together, the video producers used an impressive total of 877 images of all types (with some repetition), including many portraits, ships in action, ship models, and military/naval artifacts. The published version of the text of this historical video, entitled The Naval War of 1812-1815, provides a narrative of how the United States waged a war against Great Britain and managed to survive with such a flair that many Americans felt with confidence that they were in a new era. They had confirmed their independence, would build a larger army and navy, were free to extend maritime trade around the world, and could now claim their destiny as a democratic republic in a war-weary world.

Foreword

CHAPTER ONE

The Why, What and Who

Why the War of 1812 – 1815 is Relevant Today

The first self-awareness as a nation state for both the Americans and Canadians is rooted in the War of 1812-1815. The nationalism that resulted from the war became the foundation for "Manifest Destiny" in America and eventual independence for Canada in 1867 and the westward expansion of both countries.

On the anvil of war in the conflicts leading up to and during the War of 1812-1815 the maritime forces of the young American nation – the Navy, the Marine Corps and the predecessor of the Coast Guard, the Revenue Cutter Service, were hammered into the nuclei of what would become two centuries later the most powerful maritime force the world has ever known – a force for global good in keeping international sea lanes open and free and the global economy functioning.

The War of 1812-1815 taught Americans the hard way the importance of having and maintaining strong maritime forces. When the war was over they demonstrated they had learned their lesson by increasing naval expenditures to build a fleet of capital ships. It is the only time in American history this has ever happened.

What Was It All About?

In order to understand why the War of 1812-1815 happened, one has to go back over twenty years before the war to find its root cause: A revolution in France that plunged Europe into two decades of the most severe fighting the world had ever experienced and which made it very difficult and ultimately impossible for the United States to maintain its neutrality and not become entangled in the death struggle between Britain and France and their allies. In the eyes of the protagonists, trading with one camp made even a neutral an enemy of the other. This led America to war first with the French and then the British.

During these prologue years leading up to the War of 1812-1815, the Barbary states along the North African coast posed another very real threat to American maritime interests in the Mediterranean. This, in fact, led the newly created Congress to authorize the construction of a number of remarkable frigates that were first used against the French in the Quasi-War of 1798-1800 and then in the First Barbary War 1801-1805. These naval conflicts with the French and the Barbary states provided the newly created Navy, Marine Corps and Revenue Cutter Service with invaluable experience when they engaged Great Britain in the War of 1812-1815.

The Why, What and Who

War resulted from continued refusal by Great Britain to honor American right to free trade as a neutral and its aggressive campaign to "impress" thousands of American sailors into the Royal Navy in order to address its severe manpower shortages. In addition, some Americans on the frontier believed that the British were actively supporting Native Americans in their resistance to American westward expansion.

Who Are the Real Winners?

This book follows the conflict into its three principal theaters: First, the oceans of blue water; second, the Great Lakes and waters along the northern border of the United States; and, third, the brown waters of American coastal bays, estuaries, rivers and sounds. It concludes with a brief review of the two centuries following this formative experience that shows how American maritime forces developed from this foundation into their leading global roles today.

War on Blue Water

In the opening months of the war it is clear that the U.S. Navy bested the Royal Navy on blue water. The Royal Navy had centuries of naval experience and very rarely lost a one-on-one naval engagement with a ship of equal rating. Therefore is it not evident that America was the "winner" when, in such engagements, it captured or sank five British warships in a row? And was it not all the more remarkable a performance when a navy of no more than two dozen ships delivered such blows to one with a fleet of over six hundred? But what happened when the Napoleonic War ended in early 1814 and the British could show their true strength by redeploying men and ships to deal with these troublesome Americans? How effective was their blockade of American ports? Were some American ships able to run it? Who were the "winners" and "losers" in those situations?

War on the Lakes

The second theater of the war was along the northern border of the United States, which was naturally defined by a necklace of lakes connected by a string of rivers. Were not the British in North America (the Canadians) the winners early on when they not only stopped an American invading army but also captured it on American soil? This resulted in part from the fact that the British controlled the Great Lakes. The first "arms race" in the history of the young Republic occurred there as Americans sought to take naval control along that border. Who "won" that arms race on Lake Ontario or was it just a draw and more a "battle of the carpenters" than a naval contest?

On Lake Erie, in spite of the seesaw activity of the respective armies across the border, was it not, in the end, the American naval victory on Lake Erie that determined the outcome? Or was it the Battle of Plattsburg on Lake Champlain when the American Navy defeated the Royal Navy and thereby prevented a massive British army, battle hardened in the Napoleonic War, from invading the United States straight down the Hudson Valley? As the thousands of British retreated back to Montreal, is there any doubt who was the winner?

Ultimately, weren't the Canadians, whom the Americans outnumbered ten to one, the real winners when they successfully defended their lands from Yankee aggression? Who were the biggest "losers?" Were they not the Native Americans whose federation and alliances disintegrated when their great leader Tecumseh was killed in battle and when the British no longer could nor wanted to arm them with guns and ammunition to stop the westward expansion by American settlers into their lands?

War on Brown Water

This chapter examines activities along the coast of Maine, in Long Island Sound and in the Chesapeake Bay before turning to the last major event of the war, the Battle of New Orleans. Is there any doubt that the British clearly "won" control over the whole eastern half of the Maine coastline and kept it until the war was over? Did the Americans even try to recover it? Although in Long Island Sound the British bombarded towns, burned fleets, captured ships and successfully blockaded shipping for the balance of the war, did they "win?" Or were the "winners" the scrappy local Americans who prevented the British from establishing a base of operations in Long Island Sound as they did in Maine and in the Chesapeake Bay?

By the summer of 1814, the British were moving significant military resources from Europe to finish off the Americans who were already greatly weakened by the economic impact of the ever-tightening British blockade. Americans in the Chesapeake Bay took a serious beating. This was a much more ugly form of warfare which the British insisted they learned earlier from the Americans who had burned whole towns and had driven residents out into the dead of winter empty-handed along the northern border. After a summer of capturing ships and burning, bombarding, and blockading towns in the Bay, the British took Washington and burned the public buildings. Was this not a British "victory?"

On the other hand, the Americans successfully defended Baltimore and the British retreated from the Bay within days of failing to subdue Fort McHenry that protected Baltimore. In spite of all of the pain and suffering, who was left in control? Was it not a clear victory? And if not, how can anyone argue that the next and final major battle in New Orleans was not only a victory for the Americans but one of the most humiliating defeats for the British who had put into the battle the troops that had defeated Napoleon and the armies of Europe?

Yet, when the dust settled, was not the biggest victory for the Americans the Peace Treaty of Ghent? Through brilliant negotiation and a great deal of good fortune and luck, the Americans amazingly were left with everything they had when the war began. Yet months before the war ended, the Americans had nearly gone bankrupt as the result of the British blockade and resulting economic paralysis.

Nonetheless, in the end, Americans came to think they had indeed won the war. This was largely because of the singular victories on blue water by the American Navy, Marines and Revenue Cuttermen and the naval victories on the Lakes coupled with the lopsided and very colorfully "American" victory in New Orleans. There, General Andrew Jackson had hammered together a fighting force of pirates, freed slaves, Native Americans, Cajuns, riflemen from the hills of Tennessee and Kentucky, local militia and men from the U.S. Army and U.S. Navy and took on the world's most formidable military force. And they won. In addition, the sudden economic turnaround after the war, leading to the "Era of Good Feeling," helped everyone come to his own conclusions about the events that had just happened.

In the perspective of time, two centuries later, the clear "winner" in the War of 1812-1815 is the world today. What grew out of the tri-party war was an ever-strengthening alliance of those same three parties: The United States, the Dominion of Canada and the United Kingdom. Over the intervening two centuries, especially during the Twentieth Century and early Twenty-first, this alliance has been at the core of international forces that have fought wars to defend freedom and democracy and have kept the sea lanes free and open to international commerce of all nations – a fundamentally important fact when 70% of the globe is covered by water, 80% of its people live near the water and 90% of its commerce travels on water.

CHAPTER TWO

Prologue to War:
The Causes of the War and the Development of the United States Maritime Forces

"The United States is a maritime nation. This has been a fact throughout our history and remains very much the case today.

The oceans connect us to the world, and they sustain our trade and economy. For the past 200 years, the world's oceans have also witnessed the presence and the growth of the United States Navy and Marine Corps. On the waves, we have become what we are and will remain: the most formidable expeditionary fighting force the world has ever known.

NAVAL WAR OF 1812 -1815

It is a journey that began in earnest during the War of 1812, the first true global conflict of our still young and expanding nation."

The Honorable Ray Mabus
Secretary of the United States Navy
From the *Preface* of Yardarm to Yard 2012

In the wake of the American Revolution, the United States endured a period of great uncertainty. Although the thirteen united colonies had successfully won their independence, the new nation remained fragile and faced a number of unresolved matters. In an effort to address these issues, a convention was held in Philadelphia in the summer of 1787 during which the old Articles of Confederation were replaced by a new Constitution that vested considerable authority in the new centralized federal government, outlined the guaranteed rights of the American people and provided for the common defense. Initially, this amounted to a small standing army but no maritime force to protect the nation's coastal waters or its merchant marine in an era when the vast majority of goods moved on water. Soon there would be a need for maritime forces to protect this commerce because only weeks after George Washington, the first President under the new Constitutional system, was inaugurated in April 1789, the French people, inspired in part by the American Revolution, stormed the Bastille in Paris, beginning the French Revolution. That Revolution plunged Europe into nearly a generation of unprecedented warfare that left an estimated five million people dead. (In 1789 the entire American population was less than four million.) Had these wars not occurred, there would have been no "War of 1812" in the United States. They were the root cause of it. Out of the turmoil of this era the precursor of the United States Coast Guard emerged and the United States Navy and Marine Corps were born.

Born of Necessity

President Washington and the second President, John Adams, sought to avoid being entangled in these European conflicts. Political parties arose at this time in American politics with Adams and Treasury Secretary Alexander Hamilton leading the Federalists. This was a commerce-oriented, New England-centered party that favored sound fiscal policies, a national bank, a strong federal government and a robust Navy. They followed a policy of neutrality supported by diplomacy but also a naval program of military preparedness. A ten-year treaty negotiated with Great Britain just after the European hostilities began, the Jay Treaty, enabled Americans to ply the seas freely. American commerce increased dramatically in large part because the war swept much of the French and British carrying trade from the seas.

Since most United States government revenue came from tariffs on shipping commerce, federal coffers benefitted accordingly. To watch over these revenue activities, Congress established in the spring of 1790 the Revenue Cutter Service within the Treasury Department and authorized Treasury Secretary Hamilton to construct ten armed cutters. For nearly a decade, these Revenue Cutters enforced tariff laws and provided the nation's only naval defense.[1]

For a number of years in the Mediterranean, pirates from the Barbary states along North Africa had been raiding American shipping. To deal with this threat, Congress passed and President Washington signed the Naval Act of 1794 creating the United States Navy. It authorized the construction and manning of a number of frigates and the purchase of materials for larger ships of the line. As these ships came off the ways, Congress formally established the Department of the Navy on April 30, 1798 and the Marine Corps three months later on July 11.

---

[1] In the parlance of the day, a "cutter" was a small, fore-and-aft rigged vessel usually with single mast and a bowsprit and carried two or more head sails. The name stuck and to this day the Coast Guard, which arose from the Revenue Cutter Service, still calls its ships Cutters.

These frigates became the core of the new Navy and six would become famous in the War of 1812 – 1815. Joshua Humphreys, who ironically was a Quaker, designed them. Long in keel and narrow in beam, they were built to outmatch lighter European frigates by using heavy planking coupled with an innovative diagonal scantling to reduce hogging from the additional weight. They had the lines and carried the canvas to outrun higher rated ships of the line such as the British and French 74s. Three carried 44 guns. The ***U.S. Frigate United States*** (44) became the first ship of the new United States Navy when launched in Philadelphia on May 10, 1797. Others followed:

The ***U.S. Frigate Constellation*** (38) was built at Fells Point, Baltimore under the direction of Colonel David Stodder and launched September 7, 1797.

The ***U.S. Frigate Constitution*** (44) was built at the Edmund Hartt yard in Boston and launched on October 21, 1797.

The ***U.S. Frigate Congress*** (38) was built in Portsmouth, New Hampshire by James Hackett and launched August 15, 1799.

The ***U.S. Frigate Chesapeake*** was designed to be a 44 but material shortages and budget problems cut it down to a 38. Built by Josiah Fox at the Gosport Navy Yard in Norfolk, Virginia, it was launched on December 2, 1799.

The ***U.S. Frigate President***, the third 44-gun frigate, was built in New York City under the supervision of Foreman Cheeseman and launched April 10, 1800.

Hammered into a Fighting Force on the Anvil of War

Federalist diplomacy generally worked with Great Britain in the 1790s but France was a different situation. The United States still owed France debts from the Revolutionary War but was slow to repay them, arguing that they had been lent by the overthrown French monarchy, not the new Revolutionary government. Moreover, the French viewed American trade with Great Britain that was facilitated by the Jay Treaty akin to supporting the enemy. In the closing years of the Eighteenth Century, French privateers and even warships began to attack

American shipping, largely in the West Indies. Diplomatic efforts to resolve these matters failed so the Navy sent several of its vessels to patrol the southern coasts and the Caribbean. The best known of the several naval engagements during this two-year war involved the ***U.S. Frigate Constellation*** (38) under Captain Thomas Truxton.

On February 9, 1798 while patrolling the Caribbean off the island of Nevis, the ***Constellation*** encountered and pursued ***L'Insurgente*** (36) a French frigate under Captain Michel Pierre Barreaut. After a hard fought hour and half running battle, ***L'Insurgente*** struck, having lost seventy of its crew to the ***Constellation's*** three. The captured ship was taken into the American Navy. Two years later on January 31, 1800 in the waters off Saint Kitts, the ***Constellation*** still under Captain Truxton encountered another French frigate, the ***Vengeance,*** under Captain Pitot and gave chase, eventually engaging it in night action. After suffering much damage, it escaped under the cover of darkness. The estimated casualties were 160 for the French and forty for the Americans.

Although the Quasi War was short, it brought the U.S. Navy significant victories and prizes and the resulting Convention of 1800 resolved many of the issues between the two countries. One reason the French settled the dispute with America was that they had other more pressing matters. Under Napoleon Bonaparte the French invaded Egypt in 1798, hoping to weaken Great Britain by severing its land bridge to its empire in India and the East. However, in one of the most daring attacks in naval history British Rear Admiral Sir Horatio Nelson sailed his fleet into Aboukir Bay at sundown on August 1, 1798 and over the next two days captured all but two ships of the French fleet. There were an estimated four or five thousand casualties in the Battle of the Nile, including over one thousand killed when the French 120-gun flagship, ***L'Orient***, dramatically exploded at night. With supply lines cut, the French retreated and in 1801 the belligerents negotiated a truce, the Treaty of Amiens, and during its two-year existence the British and French abuses of American sailors' rights and free trade greatly abated. Shortly thereafter France, in need of funds to continue its wars, sold the Louisiana Territory to the United States for fifteen million dollars, doubling the size of the country. The purchase also included New Orleans at the mouth of the Mississippi, where the last major American victory in the War of 1812 would occur in 1815.

For many years the Barbary States (present day Libya, Tunisia, Algeria and Morocco) had been demanding and receiving ransom and tribute payments from the United States in order to guarantee protection of American ships and seamen in the Mediterranean. These grew in size and by 1800 constituted a significant percentage of the total revenues of the federal government. The burden was tolerated because it was thought cheaper to pay tribute than fund a naval military solution.

However, Thomas Jefferson, the newly inaugurated third President, refused to pay. Thus rebuffed, the (Libyan) Pasha of Tripoli Yussef Karamanli declared war in May 1801. Jefferson sent a U.S. Naval force to the Mediterranean including the ***U.S. Brig Enterprise*** (12) under Lt. Andrew Sterett that engaged and defeated ***Tripolitan Corsair Tripoli*** (14) on the first of August just west of Malta where it then made port. The following year Jefferson built up the Navy's Mediterranean presence with some of its finest ships and captains under the overall command of Edward Preble on his flagship the ***U.S. Frigate Constitution*** (44). These ships and men became hallmarks of the War of 1812 - 1815: ***Constitution*** (44) under John Rodgers, ***Constellation*** (38), ***Congress*** (38) under Stephen Decatur, ***Chesapeake*** (38) under Richard Morris, ***President*** (44) under Richard Dale and Samuel Barron, and ***U.S. Brig Argus*** (18) under Isaac Hull. Other ships saw duty there: the ***U.S. Frigate Essex*** (32), ***U.S. Brig Syren*** (later ***Siren***) (16), the ***U.S. Ketch Intrepid*** and the ***U.S. Frigate Philadelphia*** (36) under Captain William Bainbridge. The Navy used Sicily as its base of operations to refit and replenish provisions.

The ***U.S. Frigate Philadelphia*** grounded on shoals off Tripoli in 1803 and was captured, refloated and taken into service by the Tripolitans. That same year the ***Enterprise*** captured the ***Tripolitan Ketch Mastico*** and renamed it ***U.S. Ketch Intrepid***. The following year Commander Preble sent the ***Syren*** and ***Intrepid*** on a daring and successful raid to destroy the ***Philadelphia*** anchored in the harbor under the guns of Tripoli. With men from both ships Stephen Decatur took the ***Intrepid*** under the cover of darkness into the harbor, boarded the ***Philadelphia***, subdued the crew, torched the ship and escaped. This was a mission so unusual that British Admiral Nelson reportedly acknowledged it as the "most bold and daring act of the age."

After continued military action a peace treaty was signed in 1805, bringing an end to the First Barbary War. The following year other pirates attacked the ***U.S. Brig Enterprise*** (12) off Gibraltar but it beat them off and eventually returned home after an impressive six-year tour of duty in the Mediterranean. Over the following years the Barbary states resumed their old ways but in 1815 the U.S. Navy put an end to these annoyances in the Second Barbary War.

A New Century with Renewed Harassment of American Ships and Sailors

The opening years of the Nineteenth Century saw significant political changes both in Europe where Napoleon named himself Emperor and in the United States where Thomas Jefferson as the leader of the Democratic-Republicans (an anti-Federalist party) and his Presidential successor, James Madison, orchestrated a policy sea-change. Unlike the Federalists who championed commerce and military means to protect it with a strong Navy, the Democratic-Republicans favored an agrarian economy, defense retrenchment, reduced taxes and reduction of national debt. Relying on state militias for defense, they cut the national Army by forty percent to only 3,300 men and, following the First Barbary War, laid up Navy ships and scrapped the Federalists plans to build ships-of-the-line.

NAVAL WAR OF 1812 -1815

Harassment of American ships and sailors during the second decade of the Napoleonic Wars began again in 1803 when war resumed between France and Britain. The new difficulties were compounded for Americans by the expiry of the Jay Treaty that had provided a degree of understanding between Britain and the United States about the rules governing neutrality.

In 1805 both Britain and France reconfirmed their respective strengths when Admiral Lord Horatio Nelson defeated the combined Spanish and French fleet off Spain's Cape Trafalgar, while just days before, Napoleon triumphed at the important Battle of Ulm in Germany and days after Trafalgar he conquered the Russo-Austrian armies in one of his greatest victories, the Battle of Austerlitz in Austria. Trafalgar was a monumental victory for the British but it cost Nelson his life. He was commanding his fleet aboard the 100-gun three-decker ***H.M.S. Victory*** and engaged with the French ***Redoutable,*** a 74-gun two-decker under Captain Jean Jacques Lucas, when he was hit by a sharpshooter in its fighting tops. The ***H.M.S. Temeraire***, another 100-gun three-decker, joined the fight against the ***Redoutable*** and after hours of lop-sided battle, it struck having lost three quarters of its officers and crew dead or wounded, many of whom drowned when it sunk the following morning.

For the United Kingdom, the Napoleonic War was a high-stakes endeavor one in which the rights of neutral powers were easily ignored if need be. Witness the unprovoked Royal Navy attack on the Danish and Norwegian fleets in the 1801 Battle of Copenhagen. Viewed in this perspective, the debate between the United Kingdom and the United States and the methods employed by Parliament to try and restrict American trade, collectively known as Orders in Council, would appear almost civil. But Americans saw the situation very differently.

The Orders in Council outraged the Americans. The British had blockaded France and all its European allies. Any vessel not complying with these Orders was seized and the goods aboard condemned. In retaliation, Napoleon issued the Berlin Decree, which created a paper blockade around the United Kingdom and subjected any ship trading with it to seizure and condemnation. The difference between these blockades was simple: The British could enforce theirs while the French could not and thus most harassment the Americans experienced was with the British. Americans believed that the British had violated the Law of Nations and had no right to interfere with American international trade.

Historian Professor Donald R. Hickey estimates that on average the British and French took two hundred American ships annually between 1803 and 1812. While this is a great number, he reckons it was less than five percent of American shipping. Nonetheless, American merchants and their allies in Congress were furious. In addition, as Americans expanded settlements in the Northwest Territory (present day Michigan, Indiana, Wisconsin, Illinois) and in the Mississippi Territory (Mississippi and Alabama), they became more outspoken about raids by Native American tribes. They believed the British were behind all of these activities, supporting them with guns and ammunition. This constituency would be an important part of the "War Hawks" who called for war with Great Britain.

The issue causing the greatest tension between the United States and the United Kingdom was impressment. To meet the demands of war, from 1793 to 1812 the Royal Navy grew from over 100 ships to nearly 600 and from less than 40,000 Sailors to over 110,000. During this same period nearly 100,000 Royal Navy Sailors perished, most from accident or disease. The work was dangerous, pay poor, discipline harsh and desertion common (500 a month) so impressment became necessary to fill out crews. Impressment provided an estimated fifty percent of the Sailors in the Royal Navy in this period. Admiral Nelson mused that without impressment he had no idea how the British fleet could be manned.

The British impressed an estimated 6,000 to 10,000 sailors from American ships during its wars with France. In defense of these actions the United Kingdom doggedly maintained that the

Royal Navy was merely recovering deserters and enforcing the British doctrine of perpetual allegiance that denied the right of anybody born in Great Britain to become a naturalized citizen of another nation. The vast majority of impressments occurred on merchant ships but there were even some involving ships of the U.S. Navy. Four touchstone events along the path to war were, at root, confrontations over impressment. These were: The ***Baltimore*** incident, the ***Leand*****er** "Murdered Pearce" outrage, the ***Chesapeake-Leopard*** affair, and the ***President-Little Belt*** conflict.

Stepping Stones to War

On November 16, 1798 two British frigates halted the ***U.S. Sloop-of-War Baltimore*** as it was convoying a small fleet of merchant vessels into Havana. Its captain, Isaac Philips, then allowed a British press crew to board his ship, muster his crew, and watched helplessly as the Royal Navy impressed fifty-five men enlisted in the service of the United States Navy. Although fifty seamen were eventually returned, Philips was dismissed from the Navy for allowing such a gross insult to the American flag.

Several years later, on April 25, 1806, three British ships, including the ***H.M. Frigate Leander*** (50), were stationed off Sandy Hook, New Jersey enforcing the Orders in Council and impressing seamen. When the American cruiser ***Richard*** refused to heave to for the ***Leander,*** the British frigate fired on the American merchantman and killed one of its crewmen, John Pearce. "Murdered Pearce" became a martyr. President Jefferson banished the ***Leander*** and the other two ships from ever entering American waters again while the most rabid Anglophobes began to talk of war.

The ***Chesapeake-Leopard*** Affair nearly did lead to war. In March 1807 three men enlisted in the U.S. Navy to serve on the ***U.S. Frigate Chesapeake*** (38) in Hampton Roads, Virginia. The Royal Navy appealed for the return of these men as deserters from British service, but ***Chesapeake's*** skipper, Commodore

James Barron, refused since each was an American and each claimed to have been impressed into the Royal Navy. Months later on June 22, when the ***Chesapeake*** put to sea bound for the Mediterranean, the ***H.M. Frigate Leopard*** (50) approached it off Cape Henry. The captain of the ***Leopard***, Salusbury Pryce Humphreys, sent Barron a thinly veiled threat to give up the three deserters. Again Barron declined to do so and his refusal was met with a series of broadsides from the ***Leopard***. The ***Chesapeake*** was unprepared for hostilities and Barron quickly ordered the colors struck, but not before three Americans had been killed and another eighteen wounded. The British then boarded and took off the three they sought, all of whom were Americans plus Jenkin Ratford who was British-born and had deserted from the ***H.M.S. Halifax***. Ratford was returned to the ***Halifax***, tried and hanged from its yardarm two months later. Although much of the nation cried out for war, President Jefferson instead again tried diplomacy but, making no progress on that front, decided to bring America's economic weight to bear by cutting off American exports in the Embargo Act of 1807 and subsequent Non-Intercourse Acts. But these not only failed to bring the British to the negotiating table but also caused considerable economic hardship at home and sharpened political division.

One of the most notorious British vessels involved in impressment and enforcing the Orders in Council was the frigate ***H.M. Frigate Guerriere*** (38) that patrolled the waters around New York Harbor. In May 1811, Commodore John Rodgers was ordered to take up his station in New York with the ***U.S. Frigate President*** (44) in hopes of driving off the ***Guerriere***. En route on May 16, 1811, Rodgers fell in with another vessel that he mistook for the ***Guerriere*** and when the ship fled, Rodgers pursued. By the time Rodgers caught his chase, it was past dark and he could not observe the identity of his prey. When the Commodore hailed the other vessel inquiring as to its identity, he was met with cannon fire. Rodgers responded. After several minutes, the ***President*** silenced the guns of its foe. In the morning, Rodgers learned the ship was ***H.M. Sloop-of-War Little Belt*** (20) and the damage he had inflicted was severe: eleven British seamen were dead and another twenty-one were wounded. It was England's turn to be outraged, but most Americans viewed the ***Little Belt*** confrontation as chastisement for the ***Chesapeake*** affair.

A Divided and Unprepared Nation Goes to War

On June 1, 1812, President James Madison, leader of the Democratic-Republican Party who had been inaugurated President in March 1809, delivered a message to Congress. After days of closed-door deliberation, Congress voted fifty-nine percent in the Senate and sixty-two percent in the House to go to war. This was probably the narrowest vote on a formal declaration of war in all of American history. The vote on war was largely along party lines, with Democratic-Republicans voting for war and Federalists voting against "Madison's War" and the resolution might not have passed but for outspoken "War Hawks" in Congress from the South and West. On June 18, 1812 Madison signed the measure and the United States was at war with Great Britain. Five days later, in a seemingly unrelated move, Emperor Napoleon invaded Russia with his *Grande Armée* of 600,000 men. His failure to take Moscow, his long disastrous winter retreat by year end and his own ultimate defeat in 1814 set the stage for Britain, freed of the European war, to deliver devastating blows in America during the closing chapters of the War of 1812 - 1815.

It is a wonder the young Republic survived its decision to go to war. Fundamental problems, many long recognized before, surfaced early in the two and half years of the war. The American Army, which had been reduced by the Democratic-Republicans when President Jefferson took office at the turn of the century, had few officers with any recent military experience and many political appointees. The nation looked to state militias for defense and some of the states were so opposed to the war they refused to muster their militia when the President commanded and others, when mustered, refused to leave their state or invade British North America (Canada). The Navy was a shadow of what it would have been if the Federalist policies of the 1790's had been pursued by the Democratic-Republicans. But they "laid up in ordinary" (mothballed) blue water capital ships while they built their brown water, gunboat navy.

Importantly, since the federal government's revenues derived largely from tariffs on trade, years of trade restrictions, embargoes and harassed sea-lanes took their toll on the American economy and the government's ability to pay for the war. In 1790 the value of imports was approximately $24 million and the tariff on them totaled $3 million. In 1807 imports had risen to $145 million and tariff revenue to $27 million. However following the self-imposed 1807 Embargo, trade dropped to $58 million and tariff revenue to $11 million. In spite of doubling the tariff rates at the beginning of the war, the blockade cut import trade to $13 million and tariff revenue plummeted to a mere $4 million. All of this brought the country to the brink of bankruptcy by 1814, a situation saved only by a few individuals who provided needed funds. It also heightened domestic unrest and partisan division on many fronts. The first instance of this occurred only three days after war was declared when the largest of three deadly riots broke out in Baltimore, pitting Democratic-Republicans against Federalists presumed to be British sympathizers. More unrest and division would follow in one form or another throughout the war.

In spite of these economic and social difficulties on the home front and lack of leadership in executing the war, the Navy and Marines, even though stunted by Democratic-Republican policies, were in a much stronger position than the Army for they still had a number of ships and their officers and men had garnered invaluable experience and built an *esprit de corps* in the Quasi War with France and the First Barbary War in the Mediterranean. Moreover, in marked contrast to the Royal Navy, the men in the American Navy and Marine Corps chose to serve. They were all volunteers. They and their ships had proven themselves under fire before and were prepared to do so again.

The limitations of communication greatly complicated both diplomacy and war in the early Nineteenth Century and played havoc in the War of 1812 - 1815. News of the Declaration of War first reached London six weeks after the fact. The British had announced their intention to cancel the Orders in Council (but not impressment) two days before the Americans declared war and formally did so five days later. The British knew this news would take weeks to reach Washington so they allowed additional time for news of a hopefully favorable American reaction but eventually hearing none, the United Kingdom formally authorized general reprisals against the United States on October 13. That was nearly four months after the Declaration of War and the repeal of the Orders in Council.

The same sort of complications caused by slow communications occurred all through the war and continued after the peace treaty was signed on Christmas Eve, 1814 in Ghent (a Flemish neutral town in modern day Belgium). Even after it had been ratified and proclaimed by both belligerents on February 17, 1815, it took another four months after that for the last American Navy ship, still capturing ships on the other side of the globe, to learn that hostilities had ceased.

CHAPTER THREE

War on Blue Water, Part I:

Early American Naval Victories

The United States went to war on June 18, 1812 and the battle cry of the nation was "Free Trade and Sailors' Rights." It was largely on blue water that the United States maritime forces and American privateers found their greatest success in the "Second War of Independence with Great Britain." Most of these victories occurred in the early months of the war before the United Kingdom realized the power of the American frigates and the competence of American gunnery and seamanship and before it could devote naval resources to the American theater from the hard fought European wars. When they eventually did and began to blockade American ports, warfare on blue water by the Americans greatly diminished.

The naval war opened in June when the ***United States Revenue Cutter Thomas Jefferson*** was the first to capture a British merchantman. However, the tables soon turned against the Americans when the British took the ***U.S.R.C. Commodore Barry*** (6) on August 3 and the ***U.S.R.C. James Madison*** (10) on August 22. However, by that time, the United States Navy had joined the fray. U.S. Navy Commodore John Rodgers had readied his squadron in New York and put to sea an hour after the news of the declaration of war reached the city from Washington. He sailed on the ***U.S. Frigate President*** (44) and had in his squadron: the ***U.S. Frigate United States*** (44) under Commodore Stephen Decatur; the ***U.S. Frigate Congress*** (38) under Captain John Smith; ***U.S. Brig Hornet*** (20) under Captain Lawrence and ***U.S. Brig Argus*** (20) under Lieutenant Sinclair. At sea they learned of a convoy bound from Jamaica to Britain and, pursuing it, encountered the ***H.M. Frigate Belvidera*** (36) under Captain Byron that was escorting the convoy. When within range, Rodgers himself used a bow chaser to fire the first shot of the war at a British frigate – a war the ***Belvidera*** did not know had been declared. It and two following shots found their mark, damaging the British frigate and killing or wounding nine men. Faced with this gunning accuracy and outmatched by two to one as the ***Congress*** closed in, the ***Belvidera*** looked doomed.

However fate intervened. When the ***President*** fired the next shot from its main battery the deck below where Rodgers was standing, the cannon burst, wounded sixteen men, including Rodgers, and did much damage. Taking advantage of this turn of events, the British made quick repairs to their damaged rigging and while making their escape used their stern guns to great effect, killing or wounding another six men on board the ***President***. Nonetheless, the pursuit continued but after jettisoning its anchors, boats and drinking water, the lightened ***Belvidera*** successfully led the Americans away from the convoy and escaped itself under the cover of darkness. It returned to the

Royal Navy's principal North American station in Halifax, Nova Scotia and informed them they were at war with the Americans. Soon the ***Belvidera***, once the pursued, became the pursuer for it was ordered to return to sea with its own squadron under Captain Sir Philip Vere Broke to find the Rogers squadron.

In spite of having served well in the First Barbary War, the ***U.S. Brigantine Nautilus (12)*** was the first American warship to be captured in the war. On July 17, on a cruise less than twenty-four hours out from New York and under the command of Lieutenant William M. Crane, it fell in with part of Captain Sir Philip Vere Broke's squadron and was captured by the ***H.M. Frigate Shannon*** (38) and ***H.M. Frigate Aeolus*** (32). Taken into the Royal Navy as the ***Emulous***, it served its new masters well taking or destroying many American ships and privateers during the rest of the war.

Ordered from the Chesapeake Bay to find the ***H.M. Frigate Guerriere (38)***, the ***U.S. Frigate Constitution*** (44) under Captain Isaac Hull, did so on July 16 but found it in the company of the same Vere Broke British Squadron. A situation clearly to be avoided, the ***Constitution*** sought to escape but there was little or no wind. Both adversaries used their ship's boats to tow their ships and wetted their sails to catch what little wind there was. A clever officer on the ***Constitution*** came up with a better idea: Aware the water was only twenty fathoms in that area of the continental shelf, he suggested kedging the ship. The ***Constitution's*** boats placed light anchors well in advance of the ship in leapfrog fashion while the crew on board kedged the ship by pulling the ship forward one anchor cable length at a time with the ship's anchor capstan. The British soon followed the example. The exhausting but successful fifty-seven hour ordeal became known as the "Great Escape" and demonstrated the seamanship and tactical cleverness of the Americans.

The people of Salem, the port city in Essex County, Massachusetts, subscribed to build the 32-gun frigate ***Essex*** in 1799 and at the end of the year presented it to the United States Navy; Captain Edward Preble accepted it. Its career would prove to be quite active – serving in the Quasi-War and in the First Barbary War - and set several precedents for the Navy including crossing the Equator and doubling Africa's Cape of Good Hope. In the summer of 1812 Captain David Porter had command of the ***Essex*** and started the war by cruising in the Caribbean. He scored the first American frigate victory of the war when he engaged the ***H.M. Sloop-of-War Alert*** on August 13, 1812. The ***Essex*** may have been the smallest of the American frigates, but it still dwarfed the ***Alert*** and the engagement was rather one-sided. When Porter returned to New York with the ***Essex*** in September, he had captured ten British prizes, including the ***Alert***. Porter's success, however, was largely overshadowed by the Navy's first marquee victory of the war.

The ***U.S. Frigate Constitution*** (44) under Captain Isaac Hull clashed with the ***H.M. Frigate Guerriere*** (38) under Captain James R. Dacres on August 19, 1812. The British frigate had left the Broke Squadron and was bound for Halifax for refitting. The engagement began around 5:00 PM and lasted nearly two hours. Within a half hour of the ***Constitution's*** initial broadside, the ***Guerriere*** had lost its mizzenmast and main yard. The two frigates engaged one another at such close proximity that at one point the ***Constitution's*** rigging entangled ***Guerriere's*** bowsprit. The crews of both vessels exchanged musket fire at close range and Captain Dacres was wounded. The ***Constitution*** briefly caught fire. Then, just after the two ships disentangled from each other, the foremast of the severely damaged ***Guerriere*** broke off and fell into the sea ("went by the board"). The ***Constitution*** then withdrew while the helpless ***Guerriere*** watched it make repairs and return to close for another broadside. Dacres had little choice but to strike his colors. In keeping with the practice of the day, Dacres offered his sword to Hull but the latter refused saying that he could not accept the sword from one who fought so valiantly.

The ***Guerriere*** was so badly damaged from the better gunnery of ***Constitution*** and its superior fire power (24 pound cannon versus the ***Guerriere***'s 18 pounders) that, after transferring the crew and wounded to the ***Constitution***, Hull put it to fire. The ***Constitution***, on the other hand, with its nearly two feet of oak planking and reinforced hull was hardly marked at all. In fact, many of the British round shots had not only failed to penetrate the hull of the ***Constitution***, but had harmlessly bounced off its sides. This led the seamen aboard the ***Constitution*** to declare that the ship had iron sides, which quickly led to the nickname still in use, "Old Ironsides."

Two months later, on 18 October 1812, two smaller vessels met in battle north of Bermuda when the ***U.S. Sloop-of-War Wasp*** (20) under Master Commandant Jacob Jones engaged with the ***H.M. Brig Frolic*** (18) under Commander Thomas Whinyates. Jones had sailed from the Delaware River on October 13 and three days out encountered a severe storm in which it lost its jib boom and two seamen who were on it taking in sail. Making repairs, Jones continued south and during the night of October 17 spied a number of ships. He pursued the fleet and on the morning of the eighteenth, he deduced that he was facing a convoy of merchantships from the West Indies bound for England escorted by the ***Frolic***. It raised the Spanish flag but Jones did not fall for the ploy. He had the favored weather gauge and put it to use coming down to engage the ***Frolic*** on a parallel, with the ***Frolic*** to the left of the ***Wasp***. Both ships were armed with carronades, a powerful gun but with limited range, so it was not until the two belligerents were within sixty yards of one another that firing commenced. But the wind and sea were up and, even though both ships had reduced the amount of sail they were carrying, especially at the deck level to reduce fire hazard, the gun decks of both ships were angled over by the wind. This meant that the guns firing on the ***Wasp*** from the lee side of the ship were angled down so far that occasionally waves broke over their muzzles. The opposite was the case on the ***Frolic*** for its cannon were fired from the windward side and thus were angled up.

Since the elevation of the carronades could be raised or lowered a limited degree, most of the ***Wasp*** cannon fire hit the ***Frolic***'s hull while most of its fire struck the masts and rigging of the ***Wasp***. Soon the ***Wasp*** was unable to work its sails and the crew and hull of the ***Frolic*** took a terrible beating. Then the ***Frolic*** fell aboard the ***Wasp***, its jib boom coming between the main and mizzen rigging of the ***Wasp,*** a position that enabled the ***Wasp*** to deliver deadly raking fire. The rough seas made it difficult for the eager Americans who were largely uninjured to leap upon the ***Frolic***'s bowsprit to board but, when they did, the Americans learned the toll of their deadly, accurate fire. Of the 110 seamen and officers aboard the ***Frolic***, ninety were either killed or wounded, as compared to the ten casualties suffered by the ***Wasp***, most of whom were in the fighting tops. It was a complete victory for Jones, but short lived. The sounds of the fight had attracted the attention of the ***H.M.S. Poictiers***, a 74-gun ship-of-the-line. With rigging and sails too damaged to escape and faced with the superior power of the ***Poictiers,*** Jones had no choice but to surrender the ***Wasp***.

One week later on October 25, 1812, the ***U.S. Frigate United States*** under the command of Commodore Stephen Decatur found the ***H.M. Frigate Macedonian*** (38) in the vicinity of the Madeira archipelago in the Atlantic 350 miles off the Moroccan coast of Africa. As the vessels closed, Decatur recognized the British frigate and cleared his ship for action. Captain John Surnam Carden of the ***Macedonian*** did the same.

Curiously, both men knew each other and their ships for they had met before the war when they had sailed their ships to Norfolk, Virginia. Captain Carden bet Decatur a beaver felt hat (probably a navy cocked hat then the rage in naval dress head gear) that his ship would best the American should they ever meet in battle. He was about to have his chance. Shortly after 9:00 AM, the firing commenced and from the beginning, Decatur dictated the action. The ***United States*** (44) rated more guns than the ***Macedonian*** (38) but this mattered little since ships often carried more guns than their rating. However, the size of the guns on the ***United States*** heavily influenced the engagement. The ***Macedonian*** was a traditional 18-pounder frigate while the ***United States*** was armed with 24-pounders. This allowed Decatur to keep his ship outside the effective firing range of

Carden's frigate while he hurled broadside after broadside at the ***Macedonian*** that was very much within range of the 24-pounders. The ***United States*** inflicted great damage but received little.

After three hours of lopsided fighting and maneuvering, only two or three round shot had struck the hull of the ***United States*** while the ***Macedonian*** had received over a hundred round shot to the hull. Several of these pierced it between "wind and water," that vulnerable part of the hull along the water line that is some times above the sea surface (or in the "wind") and sometimes submersed below the surface of the water (or in the "water"). Since the ***Macedonian*** was completely dismasted and totally unmanageable, Carden surrendered. The losses aboard the British frigate were high, with 113 casualties, roughly one third of the crew, while the ***United States*** suffered only twelve casualties. Decatur claimed the ***Macedonian*** as his prize. His crew spent two weeks repairing the British frigate sufficiently enough to sail and on December 4, 1812, Decatur entered New York harbor with both the ***United States*** and the ***Macedonian***. The City was jubilant and feted him and his crew, formally recognizing his "valor and skill in the capture of British Frigate Macedonian" with an inscribed gold case. The U.S. government purchased the captured frigate and the vessel served fifteen years in the U.S. Navy as the ***U.S. Frigate Macedonian***. However no record can be found that the cocked hat was ever delivered.

But the ***Macedonian*** lives on in history, for its figurehead (the traditional statue mounted on the bow of the ship which relates in some fashion to the ship's name) has looked over future United States Navy officers from its pedestal at the U.S. Naval Academy in Annapolis for generations. And none could be more apt for the Academy, for the "Macedonian" was none other than Alexander the Great who was tutored by Aristotle and went on to become one of the greatest commanders in history. When the Greek warrior from Macedon died at thirty-three in 323 BCE, he had conquered an empire that stretched from the Mediterranean to the Himalayas.

NAVAL WAR OF 1812 -1815

Before the close of the year 1812, the United States Navy scored one more victory against the Royal Navy in a ship-on-ship engagement. William Bainbridge took over command of the ***Constitution*** after Captain Hull's victory in August. The ***Constitution*** sailed with the ***U.S. Brig Hornet*** (20) and Bainbridge planned to capture as many prizes in Brazilian shipping lanes as possible. In particular, Captain Bainbridge hoped to capture the ***H.M. Sloop-of-War Bonne Citoyenne*** that was rumored to be loaded with over 1.5 million dollars worth of gold and silver specie. The ***Bonne Citoyenne*** was indeed in the area but safe in the Brazilian neutral port of São Salvador. Instead, Bainbridge ordered the ***Hornet*** to wait until the British ship left São Salvador while he set off to capture other prizes.

On 29 December 1812, the ***Constitution*** met the ***H.M. Frigate Java*** (38) under the command of Captain Henry Lambert off the coast of Brazil. The British captain opened the engagement with a well-aimed broadside that did considerable damage to the rigging of "***Old Ironsides.***" Bainbridge responded by firing several broadsides at the ***Java,*** but the British seemed to gain the upper hand when another broadside from the ***Java*** carried away the helm on the ***Constitution*** and left Bainbridge wounded in both thighs. The American captain ordered his crew to steer from the tiller (a below deck lever attached to the rudder) and brought the ***Constitution*** in close, at which point the ***Java's*** bowsprit became entangled with the rigging of "***Old Ironsides***." Bainbridge took advantage of the vulnerability of his opponent and fired multiple broadsides into the ***Java*** before the ships were disentangled. Nearly simultaneously, the ***Java*** lost its foremast and Captain Lambert was mortally wounded by musket fire from the Marines firing from the ***Constitution's*** "fighting tops."

"Fighting tops" were platforms located at the overlap of the mainmast and topmast. Fundamentally, they provided stabilizing rigging for the topmast as well as a means to ascend or descend on shrouds and ratlines. But during close range conflict they were used as lethal unfortified bastions from which to rain down shot on the deck of an adversary. Like Captain Lambert of the ***Java***, the famous British Admiral Nelson was killed from a French fighting top in the Battle of Trafalgar some years earlier.

Under the command of "captains of the fighting tops," men on the ***Constitution*** discharged an array of weapons. In addition to the traditional muskets and pistols, they had grenades to lob and a portable swivel Coehorn mortar, which was a small cannon with a three-inch bore that fired a billiard ball-sized cluster of grape shot that caused widespread injury. The ***Constitution*** also carried the newly invented Chambers seven-barrel repeating swivel gun. This multi-barreled gun was the first repeating weapon formally contracted for use by the U.S. military. Through an ingenious firing system, it shot twenty-five ¾ inch balls from each barrel until all 175 balls had been discharged, all in a period of a couple of minutes. The downside was that it took hours to load so extra loaded Chambers guns had to be stored aloft.

Life in the "fighting tops"involved risk. Incoming shot of all kinds designed to tear up rigging and sails as well as traditional round shot aimed to dismast a ship made life in these exposed platforms very dangerous for the Marines that manned them. But the gun crews and Marines aloft had a chance for a rest as Captain Bainbridge moved the ***Constitution*** off to repair the damage his ship had received. Meanwhile, the ***Java*** laid all but helpless in the water. After about an hour's pause, Bainbridge moved his ship into the ideal position to rake the ***Java*** when he "crossed the T" and began to fire into the length of the ***Java*** and created havoc among the gun crews on the gun and spar decks. Lieutenant Chads, on whom the command of the ***Java*** had devolved, surrendered the ship. The ***Constitution*** sustained relatively little hull damage but did receive some wounds to its masts and spars. Twelve crewmen were killed or mortally wounded and twenty-two wounded. On the Java, forty-eight died (including the captain and most of the officers) and one hundred and two were wounded. It was a valiant, hard fought battle on both sides but superior American gunnery again left its mark. After removing its crew, Captain Bainbridge burned the ***Java,*** which was too severely damaged to save. The ***U.S. Sloop-of-War Hornet*** under the command of Master Commandant James Lawrence patrolled the waters outside São Salvador waiting for the ***H.M.S. Bonne Citoyenne*** for about a month until he was driven off by a British ship-of-the-line. As the ***Hornet*** sailed north along the South American coast it captured a packet loaded with over $20,000 in gold and silver specie on February 14, 1813. Ten days later Lawrence caught sight of the ***H.M. Brig Peacock*** (18) and quickly beat the ***Hornet*** to windward in order to gain the advantage of the weather gauge.

The engagement began with the ***Hornet*** and the ***Peacock*** passing by each other on opposite tacks, no more than twenty yards apart. Although the vessels exchanged broadsides in close proximity, the ***Peacock*** fired high. As a result a few Americans were wounded but the ***Hornet*** took no real damage. Meanwhile, the broadside from the ***Hornet*** tore through the ***Peacock***, severely damaging the brig's hull. Lawrence then wore his ship in order to bring his opposite broadside to bear. Peake tried to imitate the move, but the injury to the ***Peacock***'s hull slowed the brig's movement. Lawrence brought his starboard guns to bear against the defenseless stern on the ***Peacock***. There was nothing Peake could do as the ***Hornet*** poured broadside after broadside into the British vessel. Captain Peake was killed and within five minutes the ***Peacock*** surrendered and sent up a distress signal. The brig was taking on water quickly – Lawrence sent a crew over to his prize to try and save the sinking ship, but it was to no avail. The ***Peacock*** sank so rapidly that three Americans and nine Brits attempting to patch holes in its hull were caught below deck and drowned. In fact, more men perished in the sinking of the ***Peacock*** than in the actual engagement.

The United States Navy, Revenue Cutter Service and Marines began the war at sea strongly and emerged victorious in the three major and two lesser ship-on-ship engagements. These alone would not dictate the outcome of the war but they were enormously significant both in America and the United Kingdom. Theodore Roosevelt in his first book, The Naval War of 1812, explained:

"To appreciate rightly the exultation (these victories) caused in the United States, and the intense annoyance (they) created in England, it must be remembered that during the past twenty years the Island Power had been at war with almost every State in Europe, at one time or another, and in the course of about two hundred single conflicts between ships of approximately equal force, waged against French, Spanish, Italian, Turkish, Algerine, Russian, Danish and Dutch antagonists, her ships had been beaten and captured in but five instances. Then war broke out with America and in eight months five single-ship actions occurred, in every one of which the British vessel was captured."

On 18 February 1813, George Canning, a former Treasurer of the Royal Navy and Foreign Secretary, told the House of Commons in Parliament, "The sacred spell of the invincibility of the British Navy was broken." The Admiralty strengthened the North American fleet at Halifax and ordered its captains to avoid individual engagements with the American frigates, and it tightened its blockade of American ports.

Among US Navy vessels that remained outside the blockade in spring 1813 was the ***U.S. Frigate Essex*** (now rated 36) under Captain David Porter. In the South Atlantic it captured a British Royal Mail packet with $50,000 of gold and silver on board, which left him flush with specie to use for his operations. Finding little other prize opportunity in the South Atlantic, Captain Porter decided to take the ***Essex*** into the Pacific Ocean around Cape Horn. This was another precedent for the young American Navy. The ***Essex*** arrived at the neutral port of Valparaiso, Chile on March 14, 1813 flush with specie and with two whale ship prizes taken while in route.

Over the next several months, the ***Essex*** cruised the rich whaling grounds of the Galapagos Islands that sat astride the Equator and took thirteen more whale ships, including the ***Essex Junior*** (formerly the ***Atlantic***). They then sailed west and after such a long time at sea put in for repairs at Nuku Hiva, the largest of the Marquesas Islands in French Polynesia. Island intrigue kept them in the Marquesas until early 1814 when they sailed for

Valparaiso en route home. However the British learned about the exploits of the ***Essex*** and ordered Captain James Hillyar to take the ***H.M. Frigate Phoebe*** (36), and ***Sloops-of-War Cherub*** (18) and ***Raccoon*** (18) to find the American ship. The adversaries met in Valparaiso in February. They did not engage but respected Chilean neutrality and watched each other for more than a month. The Americans were not only outnumbered but also were armed principally with carronades that were good for capturing merchantships and whalers but virtually useless against British long guns that could be devastating from a distance. Thus on March 28, the Americans attempted to escape and would have been successful had the ***Essex*** not lost a topmast in a sudden burst of wind. So crippled, their fate was sealed and Captain Porter probably knew this but fought on in vain only to surrender the ship after over sixty percent of his crew was killed, wounded or went missing. Among the survivors were Captain Porter and a midshipman who would become a famous Admiral in the American Civil War, David Farragut.

CHAPTER FOUR

War on Blue Water, Part II: The British Blockade of American Ports and Economic Lockdown

The British began to blockade American ports at the end of 1812. With so much of its naval force dedicated to the European theater and so little to spare for the American matters, a British blockade was the most effective way to bottle up the American Navy and maritime commerce and thereby cripple the American economy. The British government announced its first official blockade on November 27, 1812 to cover the mouths of the Chesapeake Bay and the Delaware River, cutting off Philadelphia, Baltimore and Norfolk along with many other port towns located along those bodies of water. Aware of the hostility to the war in much of New England and the fact that its ships were still providing vital food supplies to the British army in the Iberian Peninsula, the British first expanded the blockade south of New England on March 26, 1813 to include areas around New York City, Savannah, Charleston and Port Royal, South Carolina, and the Mississippi River. Eight months later, on November 16, 1813, the British increased the blockade to cover the entire U.S. coast from Long Island Sound to the southern limit of Georgia and around the mouth of the Mississippi River. Finally on April 25, 1814, it was extended to include the entire New England coast.

In Europe the long war was coming to an end. The victorious British and their allies marched into Paris on March 30, 1814 and within a week Napoleon abdicated. As the Napoleonic War wound down, the British were able to direct more military assets to the American theater. As the blockade noose tightened, blue water activity for American commerce and the U.S. Navy greatly diminished. But fast merchantships continued to run the blockade and there were a number of occasions when American naval vessels either ran the blockade or came out to engage the blockaders. The first of these was a disaster for the Americans.

James Lawrence had been promoted to captain following his victory in the ***U.S. Sloop-of-War Hornet*** over the ***H.M. Brig Peacock*** and was given command of the ***U.S. Frigate Chesapeake***. It was in Boston harbor where the blockade had not yet been formally proclaimed but was effectively bottled up by the ***H.M. Frigate Shannon*** under Captain Philip Bowes Vere Broke. He had taken a page from the American Navy's book and rigorously trained his crew in gunnery and for fifty-six days captured and burned merchantships attempting to enter Boston harbor. He hoped to provoke Lawrence into a fight. On June 1, 1813 Lawrence had determined to rid Boston harbor of the British frigate and put to sea flying a banner that read, "Free Trade and Sailors' Rights!"

The two vessels met at 5:30 in the afternoon in the waters between Cape Ann and Cape Cod. When the engagement opened,

Lawrence had the clear advantage. The ***Chesapeake*** had the weather gauge and every opportunity to rake the ***Shannon,*** but instead Lawrence preferred to battle the ***Shannon*** broadside to broadside. While Lawrence's decision earned him praise for gallantry among the British officer corps, in the end it cost him dearly. The initial exchange of broadsides began at approximately 6:00 PM, and the ***Shannon*** achieved greater success with each successive broadside. Within thirteen minutes, the ***Chesapeake***'s wheel had been blown away, the helmsman killed, the decks swept with grapeshot, and Captain Lawrence had been badly wounded. As Lawrence was being carried below, he gave his last, and most famous order, when he directed his crew, "Don't give up the ship!" Just months later this command was flown at the peak on Commodore Oliver Hazard Perry's flagship, the ***Lawrence***, in the victorious Battle of Lake Erie and ever since has been closely identified with the Navy. The flag now hangs in a place of honor at the U.S. Naval Academy in Annapolis, Maryland.

The ***Chesapeake***'s crew tried their best to obey Lawrence's order, but it was to no avail. The American frigate was trapped against ***Shannon***'s starboard bow and Broke gave the order for his crew to board the ***Chesapeake***. In intense hand-to-hand combat the British crew seemed to gain the advantage before the American crew rallied and began to push the invaders back. It was at this point that Broke, leading the boarding party himself, received a cutlass thrust to his head after being clubbed by a musket. However, the ***Shannon***'s crew rallied around their fallen captain and forced the Americans to surrender the ***Chesapeake.*** Although Broke's wounds were pronounced fatal, he survived but he never again commanded a ship.

The engagement between the two vessels was short. The entire affair lasted no more than fifteen minutes but it was an extremely bloody confrontation. Aboard the ***Chesapeake*** sixty men were dead and another sixty were wounded, including Captain Lawrence, who died from his wounds three days later. He was thirty-two years old. The casualties aboard ***Shannon*** were also heavy, with twenty-three men killed and fifty-six wounded.

The British claimed the ***Chesapeake*** as a prize and sailed it to Halifax where its crew was imprisoned and the frigate itself was repaired and entered into the British Navy. The defeat of the ***Chesapeake*** was the first victory over an American frigate and was welcomed news for the British.

Shortly after the loss of the ***Chesapeake***, the ***U.S. Brig Argus*** under Lieutenant William Henry Allen broke through the blockade of New York Harbor on June 18, 1813. The vessel had seen extensive action in the First Barbary War including the amphibious attack on the City of Derna, immortalized in the Marines' Hymn "shores of Tripoli," and now was charged with bringing William Crawford to France as the American Minister to the First Empire. Shortly after completing that mission, the newly promoted Master Commandant Allen took the ***Argus*** on a series of audacious raids in the English Channel and the Irish Sea. During July 1813 the ***Argus*** captured nineteen British merchant vessels, and not having extra crew to man the prizes, Allen burned most. The actions of the ***Argus*** spiked British maritime insurance rates and prompted the British Admiralty to order all available ships to hunt down the American brig. Finally, in the Irish Sea off St. David's Head in Wales, the ***H.M. Brig Pelican***, under Commander John Fordyce Maple, put an end to Allen and the ***Argus***. Both American and British reports of the incident suggest that the success of the ***Argus*** was its own undoing for the day before the battle it had taken prize a Portuguese merchant wine vessel and indulged in its cargo to celebrate before torching the ship. Early in the morning of August 14 the ***Pelican*** spotted the smoke and closed. Instead of fleeing the more heavily armed ***Pelican***, Allen chose to fight but his gunnery was not as good as usual and things went badly for him. The captured ship and crew were taken to Portsmouth, England where Allan died of his wounds. In keeping with the practices of the day, the British honored his valor and buried him with full military honors.

Three weeks later the ***U.S. Brig Enterprise*** (16) engaged and captured the ***H.M. Brig Boxer*** (14) off the coast of Maine (then part of Massachusetts). This victory was particularly significant because the British capture of the ***Chesapeake*** and death of its commander, Captain Lawrence, three months before had dampened American spirits that had previously been high from the series of unprecedented single-ship frigate victories in the opening months of the war. For the British, the defeat of the ***Chesapeake*** was reassurance that, indeed, they did rule the seas.

Perception then, as now, was an important aspect of warfare and in this regard the success of the ***Enterprise*** was doubly important. It buoyed American spirits and, unlike all previous blue water engagements, many Americans were able to witness this battle since it was fought close to the shore. This engagement is also interesting because it provides a window into the standards of chivalry that existed in that age. Moreover, thanks to a British court martial held after their hard-fought defeat, one gains a number of insights into the discrepancies between the navies of the two adversaries.

Under the command of Lieutenant Samuel Blyth, the ***H.M. Brig Boxer***, armed with twelve 18 pounder carronades and two 6 pounder long guns, patrolled the coastal waters of Maine during the summer of 1813 and had taken seven prizes, mostly small coastal vessels. The morning of September 5 the ***Boxer*** was at anchor near Pemaquid Point a few miles east of Portland. A couple of its officers had been rowed ashore by some of the crew that fine fall morning to shoot pigeons so the ***Boxer's*** complement was missing a dozen men. When the ***U.S. Brig Enterprise***, under Lieutenant William Burrows and armed with slightly more guns (fourteen 18 pounder carronades and two nine pounder long guns) was sighted, the two vessels made for each other. As they did, Lieutenant Blyth had his flag nailed to the mast stating that it would remain there so long as there was life in his body. But the winds were light and occasionally calm so it was not until mid-afternoon that they met. At 3:15, not half a pistol range apart, the engagement commenced with exchanges of broadsides. Commander Blyth was killed instantly when an 18-pound round shot tore through his body and at the same time Lieutenant Burrows on the Enterprise was mortally wounded with a musket ball. Command devolved to Lt. David McCreery on the ***Boxer*** and Lt. Edward McCall on the ***Enterprise***. At 3:30 the ***Enterprise*** ranged ahead and rounded the ***Boxer*** to rake it from stem to stern. The destruction was compounded when the ***Boxer*** lost its topmast and topsail yard, and it continued as the ***Enterprise*** poured broadside after broadside into it. At 3:45, unable to strike the colors nailed to the mast, the ***Boxer*** hailed its surrender. The mortally wounded Lt. Burrows would not go below for medical attention until he received the sword of his adversary; when he did, he stated, "I am satisfied, I die contented." In addition to the loss of its commander, the Americans suffered eleven wounded, one mortally, out of their crew of 102 men while the British lost three killed and seventeen wounded, of which four would die, from their crew of sixty-six.

Civility and chivalry, which existed far more than tales of bloodshed and destruction would lead one to believe, can be seen in this minor, thirty-minute naval encounter in the middle of the war. Royal Navy Lieutenant Blyth had served as a pallbearer for the fallen American hero, Captain James Lawrence, when the British buried him in Halifax with full military honors following the capture of his ship, the ***Chesapeake*** in June 1813. (Lawrence eventually was reinterred at Trinity Church in lower Manhattan, New York where his monument can still be seen today.) Demonstrating these attributes again while patrolling the coast of Maine on the ***Boxer***, Lt. Blyth took a coastal vessel only to find it manned by a group of ladies out for a sail. Bringing them onboard the ***Boxer***, he admonished them for taking such risks and sent them home on their vessel. Upon learning of this chivalry, the husband of one of the women, an American officer in the local militia, published an accounting of the event and expressed his appreciation to Lt. Blyth in the local newspaper.

Further evidence of honor, respect and civility was seen in the elaborate funeral ceremonies for the two commanders. They were given full military honors and laid side by side in the Portland Eastern Cemetery. Later an ***Enterprise*** Sailor died from his wounds and was buried next to the two captains. British

Captain Blyth was twenty-nine years old and the American Captain Burrows, twenty-eight. The event inspired Portland resident Henry Wadsworth Longfellow to write the poem "My Lost Youth," part of which reads:

> "I remember the sea-fight far away,
> How it thundered o'er the tide!
> And the dead captains, as they lie in their graves,
> O'erlooking the tranquil bay
> Where they in battle died."

At a banquet in New York City celebrating the victory, the following toast was offered: "To the crew of the ***Boxer***; enemies by law, but by gallantry, brothers."

The British court martial accused four men of the ***Boxer*** crew of deserting their gun but also concluded that the ***Boxer***, launched a year before the battle, was of poor construction compared to the similar sized but much heavier ***Enterprise***. The U.S. Navy agreed and did not take it into service but put it up for auction. The court also noted that the British gunnery training was inadequate, that the ordnance, particularly the British cannonade, was inferior in design to the American equivalent and that the ***Boxer's*** crew, significantly smaller than the American crew, was further handicapped when command devolved upon Lt. McCreery by the absence of his fellow officers who were off birding.

Early in the war the naval architect William Doughty, who went on after the war to design 74-gun ships-of-the-line for the Navy, created a new, heavily built class of sloops-of-war. Three of these were built in 1813: The ***Frolic,*** launched in September in Charlestown, Massachusetts; the ***Peacock***, also launched in September in New York City; and the ***Wasp***, commissioned in early 1814 in Newburyport, New Hampshire. Two of these new ships would extract a heavy toll on the British Navy and commerce.

The ***U.S. Sloop-of-War Frolic*** (22) under Commander Joseph Bainbridge slipped the Boston blockade in February 1814 and went south to harass British shipping in the West Indies. After limited success, on April 20 he encountered the ***H.M. Frigate Orpheus*** (32) and the ***H.M. Schooner Shelburne*** (6) (formerly the American privateer ***Racer***). Heavily outmatched, Commander Bainbridge attempted escape into a neutral harbor and cast the ship's guns and anchors overboard to lighten it. But it was to no avail. The ***Orpheus*** caught the ***Frolic*** fifteen miles from the sanctuary of a Cuban port and Bainbridge was forced to surrender the ship without a fight. The ***Frolic*** was taken into the Royal Navy and renamed ***H.M. Sloop-of-War Florida.***

The ***Frolic*** was lost, but the ***U.S. Sloop-of-War Peacock*** and the ***U.S. Sloop-of-War Wasp*** remained. The latter was the fifth U.S. Navy ship to bear this name. One of its predecessors was the ***U.S. Sloop-of-War Wasp*** that took the ***H.M. Brig Frolic*** in October 1812 only to be captured by a British 74 immediately thereafter. The British renamed that ***Wasp*** the ***H.M. Sloop-of-War Peacock*** when the ***U.S. Sloop-of-War Hornet*** sank the ***H.M. Brig Peacock*** February 24, 1813. And two weeks later, as if this genealogy were not complicated enough already, the U.S. Congress authorized construction of the ***U.S. Sloop-of-War Peacock*** to make up for the prize of the same name that had sunk.

It was this ***U.S. Sloop-of-War Peacock*** (22) under Master Commandant Lewis Warrington that had slipped out of New York harbor on March 12, 1814. On April 28, after cruising the Bahamas for British merchantships, he encountered the ***H.M. Sloop-of-War Epervier*** under Commander Richard Wales in the waters off Cape Canaveral, Florida. The two vessels sailed for each other, and in the forty-five minute engagement that ensued, the Americans proved superior in their gunnery once again. The ***Peacock*** and the ***Epervier*** were armed primarily with carronades, so the battle was fought at close range. The first broadsides the ships exchanged were aimed at the rigging, out of character for both, but afterwards, the Americans began to direct their fire at the hull of the ***Epervier***. The ***Peacock***'s guns punched almost fifty holes into the ***Epervier*** and the British ship quickly took on water. Commander Wales mustered the crew and ordered them to board the ***Peacock***, but the crew refused; a quarter of their shipmates were already casualties and they knew that losses aboard the ***Peacock*** must have been light. (Only two men had been wounded on the American ship.) Wales had little choice and struck his colors. The Americans took the ***Epervier*** as a prize and, managing to prevent the ship from sinking, found over $100,000 worth in specie aboard. Both ships safely reached Savannah, Georgia and the prize entered the service of the U.S. Navy as the ***U.S. Sloop-of-War Epervier.***

The new ***Wasp*** surpassed the success of the ***Peacock***. From June to September 1814, the ***Wasp*** sank two British brigs and captured another, while also taking numerous merchantships as prizes. The ***Wasp*** was under Master Commandant Johnston Blakely and he had orders to harass British shipping in the English Channel, much like the ***Argus*** had done the previous year. On June 28, 1814 after capturing seven British merchantships, the ***Wasp*** sighted the ***H.M. Brig Reindeer*** (18) bearing down on it. The ***Reindeer*** under Commander William Manners had specific orders to hunt down and capture the ***Wasp***. Unfortunately for Manners and the ***Reindeer***, the ***Wasp*** was far stronger, mounting more and heavier guns. As the two vessels approached one another, the wind nearly died, leaving the ***Wasp*** and ***Reindeer*** to fight in near calm waters. After exchanging several broadsides, it was apparent to Manners that his smaller guns could not match those of the ***Wasp*** and he ordered his men to board the American. The crew of the ***Wasp*** beat back several boarding attempts before Commandant Blakely, in turn, ordered his men to board the British ship. The Americans quickly overwhelmed the crew of the ***Reindeer*** and the only surviving British officer, the captain's clerk, surrendered the ship. The British lost more than half their number, while American losses were slight, eleven killed and fifteen more wounded. Blakely burned the ***Reindeer*** because it was so severely damaged.

After putting into port for repairs at L'Orient, France, Blakely returned to the English Channel and captured several more merchantships before encountering the ***H.M. Brig Avon*** on August 27. Like the ***Reindeer***, the ***Avon*** was outgunned by the ***Wasp***, and as in so many other naval engagements of the war, superior American gunnery made short work of the British brig. Within a half hour of exchanging their opening broadsides, the crew of the ***Wasp*** had partially dismasted the ***Avon***, holed the hull several times, dismounted a number of its carronades, and made a third of **Avon's** men casualties. In contrast, the ***Wasp's*** hull had been hit only a few times and only three men had been wounded. The **Avon** surrendered, but before the brig could be claimed as a prize three British vessels, drawn by the gunfire, chased the ***Wasp*** off. The heavily damaged ***Avon*** sank shortly after the American ship left.

The ***Wasp*** continued in the Channel, harassing shipping and eventually capturing one more Royal Navy vessel, the lightly armed ***H.M. Brig Atalanta*** (8). With only eight guns, it surrendered without a fight on September 21, 1814. The small ship sailed under a prize crew for the United States and reached Savannah, Georgia on November 4, 1814. When the ***Atalanta*** left the company of the ***Wasp*** it was the last anybody heard of the American sloop. Blakely had planned to sail for Rio de Janeiro, but the ship was lost with all hands crossing the Atlantic.

American naval activity on blue water diminished in 1813 and 1814 as the British blockade of American ports tightened. One of the best examples of this was in New York City when Commander Stephen Decatur sought to evade the blockade the British had established off Sandy Hook at the southern entrance to the City. He took his squadron consisting of the ***Frigates United States*** and ***Macedonian*** and the ***Brig Hornet*** north from the City through the treacherous tide waters of Hell Gate to gain the open ocean through Long Island Sound. Sailors must have viewed it as an ill omen when first the ***United States*** grounded in Hell Gate (but was freed in the next tide cycle) and then when lightning struck the peak of its mainmast and brought down

Decatur's broad pennant. The bolt continued down the mast into the hull, shocked but did not kill members of the crew and blasted copper plates off the bottom of the ship as it entered the water. On June 1, 1813 nearly two weeks after setting sail, the American escape was thwarted by a strong British presence they found waiting for them at the Atlantic entrance to Long Island Sound. They had to take refuge in New London on the Thames River in eastern Connecticut. The frigates were caged there until the end of the war but the ***Hornet*** managed to escape and return to New York a year and half later.

The ***Frigates President*** and ***Congress*** took advantage of heavy fog and escaped Boston on April 30, 1813 and parted ways once they reached the open sea. For five months the ***President*** harassed British shippiing in their home waters from the Azores in the south all the way to Cape North in the high latitudes of Norway and, although it captured few ships, the very presence of the feared American heavy frigate drove British maritime insurance rates up markedly. After another cruise to the West Indies, the ***President*** returned to New York where it was bottled up for nearly a year.

During the closing months of the war the U.S. Navy ran the blockade and engaged the enemy four times. On January 14, 1815 a blizzard struck the New York area and forced off-station the British squadron that had kept the ***U.S. Frigate President*** (44) under Commodore Stephen Decatur in New York for many months. Weeks before, Decatur had received orders from Navy Secretary William Jones to lead a squadron made up of the ***Hornet***, ***Peacock*** and ***Tom Bowline*** to harass British shipping on the other side of the world. Thus he seized on the opportunity to run the blockade in the teeth of the storm at night. To execute this hazardous maneuver, pilots were instructed to anchor boats bearing lanterns to mark a safe channel over the sandbar at the southern entrance to the harbor. Unfortunately, the pilots failed to do so correctly and as a result in the middle of the night in a winter blizzard the ***President*** struck the bar. For two hours Decatur and his crew fought to free the frigate while the storm battered the stricken vessel. In time they managed to do so but the ***President*** sustained significant damage.

On the following morning, the ***H.M. Ship-of-the-Line Majestic*** and ***H.M. Frigates Pomone***, ***Tenedos*** and ***Endymion*** returned to their blockading station, spotted the ***President*** trying to escape and pursued it. The ***Endymion*** was a swift vessel but the ***President*** was handicapped by the damage from the sandbar. By that afternoon the ***President*** was exchanging shots with the British and by nightfall the ***Endymion*** had closed enough to fire broadsides. Decatur knew the other British ships were closing and time was short, so he ordered his crew to load their guns with chain shot in hopes of quickly dismasting his opponent. After two hours Decatur succeeded in crippling the ***Endymion***, but the ***President*** had been badly damaged as well. Decatur sailed the ***President*** south in hopes of escaping the other British frigates, but after two hours the ***Pomone*** had closed with the ***President*** and Decatur, fully aware of his hopeless situation, struck his colors. The Americans suffered twenty-four killed and fifty-five wounded while the British lost eleven dead and fourteen wounded, all on the ***Endymion***.

The ***President*** was the third frigate that the United States Navy had lost during the war, but the frigate's defeat did little to affect the reputation of its captain, Stephen Decatur. He went on to become a member of the Board of Navy Commissioners and, in addition to his bold and daring leadership as seen in his attempt to run the blockade at night in a winter blizzard and his successful night raid years before in the First Barbary War when he destroyed the captured ***U.S. Frigate Philadelphia*** anchored in the enemy harbor at Tripoli, he is also remembered for his toast to:

"Our Country! In her intercourse with foreign nations may she always be in the right; but our country, right or wrong."

The ***Endymion*** escorted the captured ***President*** and its crew to the Royal Naval station at Bermuda, barely surviving a severe storm at sea. It was taken into the Royal Navy as the ***H.M. Frigate President*** and served until 1818 when it was scrapped but only after its design was copied to build a new, identical ship with the same name. This was probably less a tribute to American naval architecture than a political statement: "Behold one of the captured American 'heavy frigates' and remember who is the Ruler of the Seas." The new ***President*** served the Royal Navy in various capacities until 1903 when it was sold.

The ***U.S. Frigate Constitution*** (44) slipped the blockade mid-December 1814 and spent the month of January raiding British shipping in the West Indies. Captain Charles Stewart commanded the ***Constitution*** and although he had received word of the Treaty of Ghent on February 8, 1815, he knew that until Congress ratified the treaty, technically any prizes captured were still legitimate spoils of war. So he continued his hunt and near the Madeira Archipelago west of Morocco on February 20, he spotted two sails on the horizon and gave chase. He learned that the vessels were not merchantships but two smaller Royal Navy convoy escorts, ***H.M. 6th Rate Cyane*** and ***H.M. 6th Rate Levant***.

Late in the afternoon he engaged them. Combined, the two vessels had about the same number of guns as the ***Constitution*** but the American ship carried heavier cannon. As the British ships began a series of broadsides aimed at the frigate, Stewart maneuvered his ship deftly. First he concentrated his fire against the ***Levant***, forcing it out of action to make repairs, then, as night fell Stewart turned the ***Constitution*** to the ***Cyane***, which quickly struck its colors. Meanwhile, the ***Levant*** attempted to flee but the ***Constitution***, a swift ship, soon overtook it and, after delivering several broadsides, forced the ***Levant*** to surrender as well. The ***Constitution*** suffered little damage in the engagement, but twelve cannonballs were found embedded in the hull of the frigate - none of which penetrated the vessel, confirming the frigate's reputation. Stewart was successful in making a prize of the ***Cyane*** but the British recaptured the ***Levant*** as a prize crew sailed it back to the United States.

In 1828 the British launched the ***H.M. Frigate President*** whose design, as noted, had been taken directly from the ***U.S. Frigate President*** that the British had captured and scrapped. Coincidentally also in 1828 the U.S. Navy "laid up in ordinary" (mothballed) its sister ship, the ***U.S. Frigate Constitution***, in Boston where it had been launched in 1797. This was not an unusual fate for a thirty-year old wooden ship especially one vastly outgunned by the Navy's new 74-gun ships coming off the ways. The Navy ordered a survey to determine the cost to bring it back into service or to scrap it. Another of the original "six frigates," the ***Congress***, underwent the same procedure a couple years later and the Navy decided to break it up in 1835. This was the normal life cycle for a warship. But on September 14, 1830 a Boston newspaper, the ***Advertiser***, reported that "***Old Ironsides***" was bound for the scrap heap. Two days later the famous poem written by a twenty-one-year-old Harvard Law student, Oliver Wendell Holmes, appeared in the same paper. Titled "Old Ironsides," the 143-word work challenged the young country to go ahead and destroy the only surviving icon it had of the new nationalism that followed the War of 1812 - 1815. The first stanza reads:

"Ay, tear her tattered ensign down!
Long has it waved on high,
And many an eye has danced to see
That banner in the sky."

This was but the first of many efforts over the generations to keep and maintain what is now the oldest commissioned naval vessel afloat in the world. (The ***H.M.S. Victory*** in Greenwich, England is older but no longer floats.) American fascination with this ship is seen in traditional art and models, but also in a variety of other ways it has been rendered in art. These range from miniatures of models in watchcases and light bulbs to one made entirely out of highly engineered steel that measures 8.5 feet long and weighs two-thirds of a ton. At the lighter end of the weight spectrum, there are commemorative stamps including one issued at the beginning of the 1812 – 1815 Bicentennial based on an original painting by Michel Fellice Corne (1752 – 1845) currently in the collection of the ***U.S.S. Constitution*** Museum in Boston. The whole tradition is probably best summed up in a scrimshaw etching on an ancient piece of ivory showing the ship on its 200th birthday under sail being saluted by a flyover of Navy jets.

As at the beginning of the war when it took six weeks for London to learn that Washington had declared war, so too at the end of the war it took time for all parties to learn that it officially ended on February 17, 1815. Unaware of this fact, the last U.S. Navy sea engagement occurred on the other side of the world four and a half months later.

Navy Secretary William Jones ordered the ***U.S. Sloop-of-War Hornet*** (20), under Commandant James Biddle, to join a squadron led by the ***U.S. Frigate President*** to harass shipping in the East Indies. Early in 1815 the ***Hornet*** eluded the blockade and worked its way to the South Atlantic to rendezvous with the ***President***, unaware that the British had captured it. On March 23 the ***Hornet*** was near Tristan da Cunha, the world's most remote archipelago located about halfway between Africa's Cape of Good Hope and South America's Cape Horn, and there found and engaged the ***H.M. Brig Penguin*** (19). Once again, American gunnery proved superior. In twenty minutes the ***Penguin*** struck its colors and was so badly damaged that it had to be scuttled. In contrast, the cannon fire from the ***Penguin*** did little damage.

Thereafter, the ***Hornet*** joined the other ships of the squadron, the ***U.S. Sloop-of-War Peacock*** (22) and the ***U.S. Storeship Tom Bowline***. Commander Biddle put the ***Penguin*** prisoners on the ***Bowline*** and sent it to Rio de Janiero. He continued with the ***Peacock*** on his mission to the East Indies. En route, they mistakenly closed on the ***H.M.S Cornwallis*** (74) thinking it was an East India Company merchantship. They narrowly escaped. The ***Peacock*** headed in one direction and the ***Hornet*** in the other. The ***Cornwallis*** pursued the ***Hornet***, which eluded capture only by throwing overboard its heavy equipment and guns. No longer useful as a warship, the ***Hornet*** returned home while the ***Peacock*** rounded the Cape of Good Hope and sailed on to the East Indies. (Interestingly, the ***U.S. Frigate Constitution*** unknowingly delayed the construction of the ***Cornwallis*** in India when it captured the ***H.M. Frigate Java*** that was bound for India with copper sheathing for the new ship. Made of teak, the ***Cornwallis*** was built to last and saw service of one kind or another until it was broken up in 1957.)

By June, Captain Lewis Warrington and the ***Peacock*** had reached the East Indies and taken three prizes. Then on June 30 in the Sunda Straights off Java, the ***Peacock*** encountered the ***East India Company Brig Nautilus*** that announced the war was over. Viewing this as a ruse, Captain Warrington opened fire. The ***Nautilus*** struck quickly but only after sustaining considerable damage. The next morning when officials in Java confirmed what the ***Nautilus*** had stated, the Americans released the ship and left for home. After many years of diplomatic negotiation the claims brought by the captured merchantships and the ***Nautilus*** against the ***Peacock*** were finally settled in 1828. The Naval War on Blue Water was over.

The Privateers: The Other Naval Force

Privateers from all of the combating nations played a very important role in the War of 1812 - 1815. This is a fact not appreciated in large part because the whole role of privateers as a legitimate part of warfare disappeared in the course of the Nineteenth Century among world maritime powers. Many people have a vague notion that it is somehow related to piracy and therefore nothing to be proud of. Both involve seizing private property but one was legitimate and profitable while the other was illegal and carried the death penalty. Governments authorized private individuals (privateers) with a license or "Letter of Marque and Reprisal" to capture enemy vessels - usually merchantships - and bring them before an admiralty court where they would be "condemned" and thereafter could be legitimately sold. To insure the privateer played by the rules and did not begin behaving like a pirate, he was required to post a surety bond usually in sizeable denominations ($5,000 to $10,000) that the government held. The privateer and the government made money when the "condemned" property was sold. The government took a portion of the proceeds and the rest was split among the privateer's captain and crew and those who invested in the privateer vessel. Thus, unlike piracy that was universally condemned, privateering was both profitable and patriotic for they were doing the government's bidding.

Estimates vary according to different sources and means of calculation but about 1,800 merchantships were seized by American privateers during the course of the two and half years of the war or an average of two per day. Many of these were recaptured so the net figure is probably closer to 1,300 but this compares to about 250 taken by the U.S. Navy during this period. Although on average each Navy ship captured ten enemy vessels, compared to three by each privateer, what is strategically important is the greater number of privateers and thus the total number of ships the privateers took. Then consider the fact that an estimated 30,000 prisoners were taken at sea by American privateers and the Navy, which is five times as many taken on land by the Army. The British, French and British North Americans (Canadians) were just as active against the Americans. Disruption to maritime commerce was enormous.

The pennant "Catch Me Who Can" best describes these highflying, fast-to-windward privateer ships. They sought to avoid, not fight, enemy warships. Money was the mission, not war. Some privateers were legendary in their financial success. One was James deWolf, "Captain Jim" of Rhode Island, who was a former slave trader and successful business entrepreneur whose privateering made him one of the richest men in America. During the course of the war he took his swift, former slaver brigantine, the ***Yankee,*** on six cruises and captured over forty vessels worth more than three million dollars. This was big money. The smallest share of just one of these cruises went to a black cabin boy, Jack Jibsheet, and amounted to more than the Navy war hero Oliver Hazard Perry earned in a full year.

The best privateer vessels were designed to outrun any adversary and even go into an enemy's escorted convoy and cut out merchantships. The famous Thomas Boyle's ***Chasseur*** (16), known as the "Pride of Baltimore," is a good example. The

Chasseur not only racked up an impressive list of captures and repeatedly eluded the Royal Navy but it did so on England's doorstep. The audacious Boyle further infuriated the British and drove their insurance rates even higher when he sent a "Proclamation" on a captured merchantship to be posted on the door of the famous maritime insurance company, Lloyds of London. Since international maritime law stated that one could not formally proclaim a blockade unless one had the wherewithal to enforce it, Boyle's proclamation was a slap in Britain's face for it equated his pronouncement (and hence ability to enforce it) with that of the British to enforce their announced blockade of all American ports.

There are many colorful stories about American privateers. One in particular is remembered for fighting valor as well as for financial success. The brigantine ***Prince de Neufchatel*** (17) sailing under Captain John Ordronaux was becalmed the night of October 11, 1814 off the Shoals of Nantucket when the ***H.M. Frigate Endymion*** (40) under Captain Henry Hope spotted the ***Prince*** and sent one hundred and twenty men in five barges under the cover of darkness to board and take it. The twenty minutes of fierce fighting that ensued were among the bloodiest of the war. The British lost forty-nine killed, thirty-seven wounded and thirty taken prisoner – 116 of the original 120. The American crew of thirty-seven suffered over eighty percent casualties – seven killed and twenty-four wounded. To put this in perspective, three months after this fight occurred, the ***H.M. Frigate Endymion*** engaged and, with the eventual assistance of other British frigates, captured the ***U.S. Frigate President*** (44). During that two and half hour duel the British ***Endymion*** suffered twenty-five casualties versus a figure nearly five times that delivered by the crew of the much smaller ***Prince de Neufchatel*** in a matter of minutes. In the closing days of the war, the British frigates ***Acasta***, ***Leander*** and ***Newcastle*** finally captured the ***Prince*** but only because it sprung its masts while trying to outrun them.

Another successful American privateer also remembered for valiancy and courage was the 14-gun brig ***General Armstrong***. Some argue that its dogged resistance to British attacks and final battle tipped the scales of the history of the war even though it was unaware of having done so. Under a very capable Captain Samuel Chester Reid, the ***General Armstrong*** sailed from New York City in September 1814 and on September 25 put in at the neutral port of Fayal in the Portuguese Azores to take on water and provisions. On the 26th a squadron of British ships under Captain Robert Lloyd including the ***H.M.S. Plantagenet*** (74), ***H.M. Frigate Rota*** (38) and the ***H.M. Brig Carnation*** (18) arrived at Fayal to rendezvous with two other British frigates coming from Spain, the ***Thais*** and ***Calypso***. The five ships were carrying artillery, troops and ammunition as part of the large-scale attack on New Orleans planned for later that fall.

It happened that the British commander, Captain Lloyd, had a passionate distaste for privateers and, although Fayal was a neutral port and thus he could not attack the ***General Armstrong***, he could not resist. That was his first mistake because the American with its battery of long nine pounders and its one "Long Tom" cannon beat back the first attack of British boats while inflicting considerable loss. At midnight a larger flotilla consisting of a dozen armed barges with up to 400 men attacked the ninety men on the American brig. Although the attackers breeched the boarding nets and boarded the bow of the ***General Armstrong***, the Americans rallied under Captain Reid and drove them off with considerable loss of life and barges. This only infuriated the British commander who ordered the ***Carnation*** to close with the American. Not only were more British Sailors lost but also their ship was badly damaged and retreated. Records vary but the Americans lost three killed and several wounded while the British reportedly suffered sixty-five killed and 117 wounded.

As the new day dawned, the British were determined to eradicate the American nuisance. Seeing the handwriting on the wall and vastly outgunned, Captain Reid landed his men and weapons on shore, scuttled the brig and fortified an abandoned castle, daring the British to further violate the laws of neutrality by attacking on land. They did not. The British frigates from Spain arrived but, contrary to the plan to sail immediately to New Orleans, they were ordered to transport back the many wounded while repairs were made to the damaged ***Carnation***. In all, about three weeks were lost because of the ***General Armstrong*** diversion. As shall be seen later, General Andrew Jackson arrived in New Orleans just days before the British and rushed to organize its defenses. Had the ***General Armstrong*** not put up such a fight and delayed the British attack on New Orleans, who knows if General Jackson would have been victorious at New Orleans?

CHAPTER FIVE

War on the Lakes

British North America (what we know as Canada today) was thinly settled in the opening years of the Nineteenth Century. The population was about one-tenth that of the United States and, like much of America, was found in small settlements some of which were fortified. Access to rivers and lakes was key for there were few roads and most trade and supplies moved over water.

The British in North America had strategic alliances with local Native American tribes that dated back to the French and

Indian War of 1756-1763. On the other hand, the Americans, constantly pressing west into Native American lands, had much more contentious relationships with their indigenous people. The tribes were not isolated entities but were often allied or federated with other tribes on either side of the border. Moreover, some outstanding and visionary Native Americans influenced tribes throughout the western frontier, from the Gulf of Mexico to what is now northern Ontario. One such leader was Tecumseh. He was closely allied with the British who supplied him and his allies with arms and ammunition. Americans in the frontier "west" (the Northwest Territory) and frontier "south" (the Mississippi Territory) often felt the consequence of this arrangement and they seized upon the maritime conflict of the coastal states with the British as a way to address their own needs in Congress. They were known as the "War Hawks" and believed that war with Great Britain would eliminate or at least greatly reduce the threat the Native American tribes posed.

American thinking about British North America prior to the opening of war could be found in four schools of thought:

1. Merely threatening to invade Canada (a place very difficult for the British to defend) would bring the British to their senses about their abuses of American maritime rights;
2. If the threat did not work, invading and holding the thinly populated Upper Canada (present day Ontario) would provide a stronger bargaining chip at the negotiating table;
3. The British threat to America's northern border and its troubling relationship with Native American tribes could be eliminated entirely if the British were driven out and Canada, or at least Upper Canada, became part of the United States; and,
4. There was the notion that the Canadians would welcome American "liberation from the tyranny of the British Crown." This was especially naïve because many American Loyalists had fled to Upper Canada during and after the Revolutionary War.

In the early Nineteenth Century, the border that the United States shared with British North America was made up of impenetrable forests. But running through them from the

Atlantic to the middle of the continent was a water necklace that served both as a natural border between the two countries as well as the best means of transportation. Much of this necklace was made up of the St. Lawrence River that drained the Great Lakes and, flowing from the west to the east, emptied into the Atlantic at the Gulf of St. Lawrence. If one started there and headed west or "up" the St. Lawrence River for three hundred miles, one would first come to Quebec. Two hundred miles farther, one would find the town of Sorel Tracy situated at the mouth of the Richelieu River that is fed by waters flowing north from Lake Champlain. Continuing westward another eighty miles on the Saint Lawrence brings one to Montreal, and a hundred and seventy-five more, to Lake Ontario. Across it one would continue up the Niagara River and go around Niagara Falls into Lake Erie. Then one would cross Lake Erie and go up the Detroit River to Lake Huron and Lakes Michigan and Superior. These last three far-distant lakes did not figure significantly in the war although one of the first victories for the British and their Native American allies was the July 17, 1812 surprise raid and capture of Fort Mackinac, an American trading post located where Lake Huron meets Lake Michigan. It was a position they successfully held until the end of the war.

From a military point of view, the three key theaters were:

1. Lake Erie, where the Americans hoped to invade the sparsely populated "Upper Canada" from Fort Detroit located on the Detroit River in the Michigan Territory;

2. Lake Ontario where the Americans planned to invade across the Niagara River; and,

3. Lake Champlain which, when combined with the St. Lawrence River, offered the British a waterway from the more populated part of their colony directly south on the Hudson River into New York. If the British were successful in using this route, they could effectively sever New England from the rest of the United States.

Lake Erie: 1812

When the war began in June 1812, the U.S. Navy's presence

on the Great Lakes bordered on non-existent. It had no ships on Lake Erie although American forces had fitted out the ***U.S. Army Brig Adams*** (6) at Fort Detroit on the western end of the lake. The British, on the other hand, had a number of ships as part of their Provincial Marine. This was more a military transport service than a naval one and was manned by local, not Royal Navy. They included the ***P.M. Sloop-of-War Queen Charlotte*** (17), the ***P.M. Brig General Hunter*** (10), and the ***P.M. Caledonia*** (3). The ***P.M. Brig Lady Prevost*** (13), under construction on the ways, would soon join them. It was easy for the British to seize control of Lake Erie as soon as the war began.

The American Brigadier General William Hull, Governor of the Michigan Territory and Revolutionary War hero, was ordered to invade Canada from Fort Detroit. He first went to Ohio and gathered 2,000 regular and militia troops and marched across the Ohio wilderness to Fort Detroit. He knew his supply lines back to Ohio overland were in jeopardy and those over Lake Erie were virtually non-existent because of the British control of the Lake. The hope was that a quick strike from Fort Detroit and the capture of Upper Canada would make the British naval control of Lake Erie irrelevant and short-lived.

Hull was right to be concerned about the importance of sea-lanes for when the men of his army reached Fort Detroit on July 5, they found no supplies and the only U.S. maritime force on the Lake, the ***U.S. Brig Adams*** (6), under repair and incapacitated. Meanwhile Hull's land supply lines were intercepted and on July 2 the ***P.M. Brig General Hunter*** captured the American schooner, ***Cuyahoga***, in which Hull had shipped much of his important war material to lighten his march to Detroit. Nonetheless, on July 12, Hull crossed the Detroit River into Canada, made his famous Proclamation that he had come to "liberate" the inhabitants most of whom did not seem appreciative of his offer. Having no artillery, Hull did not attack the defending British fort but returned back across the Detroit River.

Worse yet, the seasoned and highly respected British Major General Isaac Brock who was in charge of the military in

Upper Canada had learned about Hull's army in Fort Detroit and its general condition and marched to put an end to this threat. Playing on the known weakness of the American situation at Ft. Detroit and fully aware of Americans' fear of Native American "savages" (a good number of whom were with Brock under Chief Tecumseh), Brock crossed the Detroit River and laid siege to the fort. He then orchestrated a masterful deception leading the Americans to believe that he had far more men and "savages" than he did. He convinced Hull on August 16 to abandon his hopeless situation in order to avoid the savagery of the Native Americans whose blood lust he might not be able to control. Hull surrendered with his entire army, and with the prizes of war went the ***U.S. Army Brig Adams***, then renamed ***Provincial Marine Brig Detroit***. This victory greatly strengthened the British hold on the Lake and not only prevented an American invasion along the western border but also put in jeopardy other American forts in the Northwest Territory.

Daniel Dobbins was a colorful and successful merchant who bought salt from mines in New York and transported and sold it throughout the northwestern region via Lake Erie and Lake Huron on his ship the ***Salina.*** But twice at the beginning of the war he was at the wrong place at the wrong time and twice the British captured him. First he was taken in a surprise raid on Fort Mackinac on July 17 along with its American defenders who did not know war had been declared. He extricated himself from that and was on his way home to Presque Isle (now Erie, Pennsylvania) on the southern shore of Lake Erie when he stopped in at Fort Detroit just when the British took it. Once again, he escaped and brought news of both British victories to his poorly defended hometown. Alarmed that Presque Isle would be the next to fall to the British and at the urging of the local militia, Dobbins made the long trip to Washington, D. C. to meet with President Madison and the Navy Department to plea for a strong naval presence on Lake Erie. After debate as to the best location to build ships in the wilderness of Lake Erie, they chose Presque Isle. It had a natural harbor and sandbar that would protect the harbor from deep-draft warships and was within reasonable proximity of the manufacturing frontier town of Pittsburgh some miles to the south. Dobbins was commissioned a Captain in the Navy, ordered to return to Presque Isle and build four ships and given funds to do so. He brought with him the shipwright Ebenezer Crosby and together they began to turn wilderness forests into warships.

Fully appreciative of the importance of naval control of the Lakes in determining the outcome of the war, the Navy was already moving on other fronts and had ordered Captain Isaac Chauncey to leave the Navy Yard in New York City and report immediately to the naval station at Sackets Harbor on Lake Ontario where he was to build a commanding naval presence to take control of Lakes Ontario and Erie. Chauncey, in turn, learned about a young Navy officer stationed in Rhode Island who had requested a transfer from a command of gunboats there to the Lakes. Oliver Hazard Perry, son of a Navy Captain, had become a Navy Midshipman at the age of thirteen and had seen duty in the Quasi-War with France and the First Barbary War. He was just what Chauncey wanted – an experienced, energetic, good administrator officer looking for action. Chauncey put Perry in charge of naval activity on Lake Erie.

Lake Ontario: 1812

When war was declared the Americans had only one naval vessel on Lake Ontario, the ***U.S. Brig Oneida*** (16), but it was under the command of Lieutenant Melanchthon Taylor Woolsey and had an experienced crew. It was based in Sackets Harbor, a weakly defended base at the eastern end of Lake Ontario in northern New York where the lake waters begin to flow into the St. Lawrence River. To the north, across the Lake, was the Kingston Provincial Marine Naval Dockyard where the Provincial Marine had an impressive fleet of six vessels, including ***P.M. Sloop-of-War Royal George*** (22), ***P.M. Sloop-of-War Prince Regent*** (16), ***P.M. Brig Earl of Moira*** (14), ***P.M. Brig Duke of Gloucester*** (10), ***P.M. Schooner Senica*** (8) and ***P.M. Schooner***

Simco (8) all under Master and Commander Hugh Earl. But they were crewed by much less experienced men. In early July 1812, Lieutenant Woolsey complained to his superiors about the lopsided situation and, as if to underscore his point, the ships of the Provincial Marine attacked Sackets Harbor on July 19. However, Woolsey was able to fend them off. This only confirmed the British conviction that they, too, needed to strengthen their naval presence. What ensued was the first naval arms race in United States history, referred to as the "battle of the carpenters." As an immediate first step, Lieutenant Woolsey was ordered to buy six schooners to convert into warships. These were the ***U.S. Schooners Hamilton*** (10), ***Governor Tompkins*** (8), ***Conquest*** (6), ***Growler*** (2), ***Julia*** (2) and ***Pert*** (1).

On September 3, the Navy placed Captain Isaac Chauncey in command of Lake Ontario and Lake Erie. Chauncey's shipbuilding experience at the New York Navy Yard was important, as his first task at Sackets Harbor was to build a substantial fleet that he was to command. This task was complicated by its remote location far from the naval stores of the Atlantic coast. While American supplies in the East were a great deal closer to the Great Lakes as a bird flies than were the British supplies at their major naval station at Halifax, Nova Scotia, water transport made it much easier for the British. The Americans had to drag materials and guns across New York State through the Mohawk valley wilderness (the future site of the Erie Canal) or haul cannon up from the Chesapeake Bay. Moreover, seasoned timber did not exist in the region, forcing Chauncey to build with green lumber. Despite these difficulties that Chauncey faced on Lake Ontario and Perry faced on Lake Erie, they enlisted hundreds of men in their efforts including Navy Sailors and Marines, carpenters and shipwrights along with the leading New York naval architects Adam and Noah Brown and Henry Eckford. They made do with what they had. They substituted tree nails (or trunnels) for iron nails and used lead that was available from mines in the west to replace oakum for caulking and pig iron for ballast.

Under Chauncey's direction they laid down the keel for the ***U.S. Corvette Madison*** (24) and purchased four more ships and armed them with cannon, the ***U.S. Schooners Ontario*** (2), ***Scourge*** (9), ***Fair American*** (2) and ***Asp*** (1). Designed to work lakes and harbors, these trading schooners had shallow drafts, unlike their deeper keeled ocean counterparts. As a consequence, once armed with heavy cannon, they tended to be top heavy and were generally poor sailors. These aspects would constantly hamper the effectiveness of the American fleet. Before the winter closed the Lake, Commodore Chauncey took the ***U.S. Brig Oneida*** and some of his ships to attack Kingston on November 6 but it was inconsequential and called off when the single cannon exploded on the ***U.S. Schooner Pert***.

Of much greater significance was the decisive defeat of what was to have been the second prong of the American invasion of Canada. This was across the Niagara River upstream from where it flows into the western part of Lake Ontario. (The first prong was Hull's unsuccessful attempt from Fort Detroit across the Detroit River at the western end of Lake Erie three months earlier.) The Americans under Major General Stephen Van Rensselaer crossed the Niagara River to take Queenston on October 13 but were repulsed and lost more than 1,000 men, captured, wounded or killed at a cost of over 100 defenders. But one of the dead at the Battle of Queenston Heights was the venerated British Major General Isaac Brock, a competent administrator and general. He became one of the great heroes in Canadian history and was memorialized with large a monument raised to his memory in 1824. Meanwhile on Lake Ontario, the British laid down keels for two 24-gun ships, the ***P.M. Sloop-of-War Wolfe*** to be built in Kingston and the ***P.M. Sloop-of-War Isaac Brock*** to be constructed in York (now Toronto) at the western end of the Lake.

Lake Ontario: 1813

The year 1813 began with a change in British leadership on Lake Ontario when Royal Navy Captain James Lucas Yeo and seasoned Royal Navy officers arrived to replace Provincial Marine Master and Commander Hugh Earl. At this point the Americans intended to launch another prong of their strategy to take Canada. The plan was to use several thousand troops of the Army under Major General Henry Dearborn in conjunction with Commodore Chauncey's growing naval strength to attack and take the Kingston Royal Navy Yard and then attack York and Ft. George at the mouth of the Niagara River. This would give a significant and perhaps decisive strategic advantage to the Americans in Upper Canada. However faulty intelligence led the Americans to believe Kingston had been greatly reinforced so they revised the plan and Commodore Chauncey sailed west with his fleet along with Dearborn's troops and an amphibious force under the command of explorer Brigadier General Zebulon Pike to capture York. The coordinated attack on April 27 went well for the Americans. Retreating and cutting their losses, the British set fire to both the ***P.M. Sloop-of-War Isaac Brock*** (24) under construction and the fort's magazine. When the latter exploded, it killed General Pike and caused nearly 250 of the total 320 American casualties. In the battle the British lost 475 killed, wounded and captured. Although peace was negotiated, the Americans burned the public buildings and plundered much of the town, contrary to orders from General Dearborn. The consequences would be costly for the Americans later on their own soil.

In keeping with their plan, the Americans then sailed south and took Fort George in another successful joint Army/Navy amphibious attack on May 25. Since the British believed the entire line of their forts along the Canadian side of the Niagara River were vulnerable following the loss of Ft. George, they evacuated them and regrouped to the west while the Americans occupied them. In the course of the summer and fall, the British Army mounted successful counter attacks at Stoney Creek (June 5) and the Battle of Beaver Dams (June 24). The success at the latter is attributed to Laura Secord whose husband was still recovering from wounds at the Battle of Queenston Heights months before and who walked through twelve miles of unfamiliar and dangerous territory to warn the British the Americans were coming. She became a national heroine and, along with General Brock, a symbol of Canadian determination to resist American aggression. As the British regrouped on land, the Americans retreated, eventually abandoning all of the captured forts along the Canadian side of the Niagara River. The year ended little different than how it had begun.

Meanwhile, back on the naval front, news of the fall of Fort George and York reached Kingston where visiting Commander-in-Chief Prevost and Commodore Yeo decided to attack Sackets Harbor while the American forces were occupied in the western part of the Lake. On May 27 British troops and ships set sail and arrived the next morning but the assault was delayed by the unexpected arrival of a flotilla of boats carrying American Soldiers to Sackets Harbor. While the British dealt with them, killing or capturing most, it gave the Americans time to rally militia and strengthen defenses to the point where the British eventually aborted the attack and returned to Kingston. Casualties totaled fewer than 600 killed, wounded or captured and were roughly divided equally between the warring parties. Strategically, the Americans set fire to the ***U.S. Sloop-of-War General Pike*** (28) still on the ways, fearing it would fall to the British. When the British suddenly left, the fire was put out and, because the ship was built with green wood out of necessity, the fire damage was limited. It was launched June 12, tipping the balance of firepower in favor of the Americans – for a while.

During the rest of the year on Lake Ontario there were a number of skirmishes, none of which were strategically significant but all of which demonstrated the caution the commanders of both navies exercised lest they lose ships and give the command of the Lake to the other party. The first was an encounter on August 10 two days after the ***U.S. Schooners Scourge*** (9) and ***Hamilton*** (10) capsized while at anchor in a sudden night squall, with the loss of most of the men aboard. The squadrons of the two adversaries met in battle formation and two American schooners, the ***Growler*** (2) and the ***Asp*** (1), failed to wear (or turn) with their fleet and the British captured them. Another, less consequential encounter was an ineffectual distant engagement off the mouth of the Genesee River east of Niagara on September 11.

But a more memorable one that has come down through history as the "Burlington Races" occurred in York Bay on September 28 when Commodore Yeo and his flagship the ***P.M. Sloop-of-War Wolfe*** (24) and a number of vessels in his squadron met Chauncey in his flagship ***U.S. Sloop-of-War General Pike*** (28) accompanied by the ***U.S. Corvette President Madison*** (24) ***and U.S. Schooner Sylph*** (12). Each towed one of the slow-sailing armed schooners. They briefly dueled during rising weather. While the ***General Pike*** was damaged, the ***Wolfe*** lost its mizzenmast and main topmast and dramatically beat downwind in a gale for an hour and half to escape the pursuing Americans. Chauncey, slowed by the dullard schooners he was towing and fearful of being driven onto a lee shore that was controlled by the enemy, called off the pursuit and Yeo anchored safely in Burlington Bay.

The final incident occurred when the Americans unsuccessfully attempted to mount another planned prong of the invasion of Canada. This involved American forces from Sackets Harbor under General James Wilkinson going down the St. Lawrence River to attack Montreal while other American forces came up the St. Lawrence from Plattsburg on Lake Champlain under General Wade Hampton to attack Montreal from the opposite direction. A number of elements combined to doom the effort: personality conflicts (Wilkinson and Hampton hated each other), poor leadership, illness, adverse weather and poor communications, not to mention a bold move by the British. Seasonal rough weather had weakened the American blockade of Kingston and a British force under Colonel Joseph Morrison slipped out aboard ***H.M. Schooners Beresford*** and ***Sidney Smith*** under Captain William Mulcaster to attack the Americans as they made their way down the St. Lawrence toward Montreal. Although only a tenth the size of the American army, they surprised the Americans at John Crysler's farm near Morrisburg on the Canadian side of the St. Lawrence River on November 11 and forced them to retreat in disarray to the American side. The plan to attack Montreal from Sackets Harbor had been frustrated and the Americans called off the campaign. We shall see later how and why the other force from Plattsburg on Lake Champlain also failed.

Lake Erie: 1813

In the fall of 1812 American Commander Isaac Chauncey, newly charged with responsibility for all naval activities on Lakes Ontario and Erie, appointed Lt. Jesse Duncan Elliott to acquire four vessels to be converted into warships for the Lake Erie fleet. Elliott went to Buffalo at the eastern end of Lake Erie and across the Niagara River from the British Fort Erie and began to buy vessels.

In early October two brigs, the ***P.M. Brig Detroit*** (6) and the ***P. M. Brig Caladonia*** (3) dropped anchor under the guns of Fort Erie. These vessels would provide an excellent nucleus for the new fleet if they could be "cut out" and brought over to the protection of American guns. Elliott conferred with Colonel Winfield Scott who was based in Buffalo and they hatched a plan to take two scows with muffled oars and dozens of men in the dead of the night on October 9, cross the river, surprise and overwhelm the crews. It worked. The ***Caladonia*** made it back to the American side safely but the ***Detroit*** got caught in the current of the river, ran aground and after attempts by both sides to retake it, the Americans managed to unload munitions that had been taken from Ft. Detroit when it fell to the British and then burned the vessel. Within months the British built a bigger ***Detroit*** that would be their flagship in the Battle of Lake Erie.

The British guns of Fort Erie effectively blockaded Lt. Elliott's new fleet in Buffalo until the Americans took Fort George on May 24 and the British abandoned all fortifications on their side of the river, including Fort Erie. At that point, Elliott and a couple hundred men and several teams of oxen towed the five vessels up the Niagara River and into Lake Erie where they sailed safely to Presque Isle. The five were: the captured ***U.S. Brig Caladonia*** (3), ***U.S. Schooners Somers*** (2), ***Tigress*** (1), and ***Ohio*** (1), and ***U.S. Sloop Trippe*** (1). When they arrived at Presque Isle they found Commodore Perry in full swing. He had arrived with his brother, Alexander, in the late winter and had taken on his new responsibility with remarkable energy and sense of urgency. Along with the imported shipwrights, naval architects and shipbuilders they had built the ***U.S. Schooners Ariel*** (4), ***Scorpion*** (2) and the ***Porcupine*** (1) and had laid keels for two large, identical, 20-gun brigs, the ***Lawrence*** and the ***Niagara.***

Across the Lake, the British under the one-armed Captain Robert Heriot Barclay, a seasoned officer who served with Admiral Nelson in the Battle of Trafalgar, oversaw a similar effort in Amherstburg (Fort Malden) to build a fleet in the wilderness. His logistics were no better and one could argue they were considerably worse than those of the Americans but nonetheless they assembled a fleet of six ships including the three large ones that, on a tonnage basis, more or less matched the three largest American ships: ***H.M. Sloop-of-war Detroit*** (20), ***H.M. Sloop-of-War Queen Charlotte*** (18) and ***H.M. Schooner Lady Prevost*** (14). They also had the ***H.M. Brig Hunter*** (10), ***H.M. Schooner Chippeway*** (1) and the ***H.M. Sloop Little Belt*** (3). These ships, with the exception of the American ship ***Ohio*** that had been sent on another mission, made up the two fleets in the Battle of Lake Erie.

Time was another enemy for Captain Barclay for provisions at his base were running low and resupplying them was increasingly threatened by the American presence on the Lake. Moreover, the British were feeding thousands of Native American allies camped at Fort Malden (Amherstberg) who would disband if food were cut off. Accordingly, Captain Barclay pressed the new flagship ***Detroit*** into service arming it with cannon taken from Fort Malden that had to be fired by igniting their touchholes with pistol fire. So readied, Captain Barclay stood to sea to meet the Americans in what would be the first fleet battle in American naval history.

In just about every way, the American fleet was larger: number of vessels (9 versus 6), tonnage (1,691 versus 1,460) and number of crew (approximately 530 versus 440). Although the British carried more cannon (66 versus 54), the broadside weight of the American guns was nearly two to one (936 pounds versus 469 pounds) and, importantly, the Americans had very heavy long guns mounted on their smaller vessels. This was a real asset in light airs as was the case in the Battle of Lake Erie. The Americans had two long 32 pounders and four long 24 pounders versus the British who had none of the former and only two of the latter. Noteworthy in terms of understanding the battle tactics, both American brigs were armed primarily with carronades, deadly but short ranged weapons, whereas their British counterparts were more evenly balanced between carronades and long guns.

The very sandbar lying six feet below the entrance to Presque Isle harbor that protected the town from large warships was, of course, a real problem when it came to getting large ships built there out of the harbor. The solution was known from the beginning but there was a twist that could have prevented success. Once ready for sea, they would "camel" the new brigs over the "camel hump" of the bar. This involved placing special barges along either side of the ship, running large timbers through its fore and aft gun ports, opening seacocks to flood and lower the barges, blocking up the ends of the large timbers on the barge decks, closing the seacocks and pumping out the water and thereby lifting the ship and lessening its draft. Once over the bar, the process would be reversed. The fly in the ointment was the fact that to lighten the brig as much as possible, its guns had to be unloaded thereby making it defenseless during the hours-long procedure. This was not a problem unless the enemy was sitting outside the harbor waiting for the camel process to begin. And, of course, the British were and they maintained a blockade watch constantly until August 4 when they inexplicably disappeared. Jumping on the opportunity, Perry got his flagship, the ***Lawrence,*** to the bar and began the camel process that afternoon. It took longer than anticipated since the brig drew too much water and the camel process had to be done twice, but by daybreak it was across and rearmed. At that time the British reappeared but it was too late. After some exchange of fire they withdrew and the ***Niagara*** cameled the bar with no problem. The Americans' superiority was no longer theoretical.

After the American brigs passed the bar, Master Commandant Perry spent a couple of weeks on a shakedown cruise during which he trained his men. Manpower was in short supply; he was unable to get any from his commanding officer Commodore Chauncey on Lake Ontario so he turned to General Harrison in charge of the Army in the Lake Erie region. He gave him any men who had sea experience plus about one hundred Kentucky sharpshooters who went on board as Marines. Ready for action, Perry took his fleet to Put-in-Bay on the western end of the lake where he waited for Captain Barclay to sail out. On September 9 he led his fleet of six ships out onto the Lake and the morning of the next day the Americans spotted them.

The winds were fickle but gave the Americans the weather gauge. Both fleets assembled in battle formation with the ***Ariel*** and ***Scorpion*** leading the ***Lawrence*** down to engage the first of the British ships, the ***Chippeway***, ***Detroit***, ***Hunter*** and ***Queen Charlotte.*** The other vessels of both fleets followed their respective flagships. At 11:45 the ***Detroit*** opened with a shot from a long 24 pounder but it fell short. Five minutes later a second struck home, tearing through the ***Lawrence***. The ***Scorpion*** replied with its long 32 pounder, thus initiating general long gun action. It took many minutes for the ***Lawrence*** to get within range to use most of its guns (the eighteen 32 pound carronades) and all the while it took concentrated long gunfire from the ***Detroit*** and ***Chippeway***.

Meanwhile, ships in the aft part of the respective columns engaged in long gun duals until the American ***Caledonia*** and British ***Hunter*** came into the main fray to aid their respective flagships. The American ***Niagara*** under Captain Elliott whose battery consisted mostly of short-range carronades remained out of range of the action. With this exception, both sides fought well and valiantly and the carnage in the thick of action was considerable. It was made all the more horrific because the shallow draft of these vessels designed for the Lakes provided no deck space below the waterline where surgeons could more safely operate and care for the wounded like in most blue water warships. Thus, they were exposed to the real killer in wooden ships, barrages of "splinters" - large, sharp slivers of wood - that exploded inward on the men when cannon balls penetrated the hull. Yet out of this ward room on the ***Lawrence*** came wounded who responded to Perry's call for help back on deck. This continued until Perry, with the assistance of the chaplain and the purser fired the last cannon. Four out of every five men Perry started the battle with on the ***Lawrence*** were dead or wounded; it was a floating but demolished wreck.

Perry reordered the line of battle for his ships and then took four men and his brother Alexander in a rowboat and transferred his flag to the untouched ***Niagara***. As the firing ceased on the ***Lawrence***, the British thought the Americans had capitulated. Soon they did and even though there were only fourteen men left standing on the ***Lawrence***, the British were unable to take possession of the ship because their own ships were so damaged and because the ***U.S. Brig Caledonia*** placed itself between the British and the drifting ***Lawrence***.

Upon taking command of the ***Niagara***, Captain Perry sent Master Commandant Elliott astern to bring the three American schooners in a closer formation. At 2:45 he led this squadron back into the center of the battle to sever Barclay's line. As Perry broke across Barclay's line he raked the British ships on both sides with devastating broadsides. Heavily damaged and no longer maneuverable, the ***Detroit*** and ***Queen Charlotte*** fell afoul of each other. Captain Barclay realized the situation was hopeless and struck his colors at 3:00 PM – three hours and fifteen minutes after he had begun the fight. The ***Chippeway*** and ***Little Belt*** tried to escape but were overtaken and captured by the ***Scorpion*** and ***Trippe***. Captain Perry scribed a report of the battle that only added to his legend: "We have met the enemy and they are ours: Two ships, two brigs, one schooner and one sloop."

The American fleet suffered a total of 123 casualties, two thirds of whom were on board the ***Lawrence***. Twenty-seven had been killed and ninety-six wounded, three of whom died. The British had 135 casualties, forty-one killed and ninety-four wounded. The first and second in command of every British ship was either killed or wounded – a testimony to their valor.

Theodore Roosevelt in his first (of three dozen) books, the Naval War of 1812 examined each battle of that war from every angle – size and makeup of weapon strength, the crew's training and capability, ship design, seamanship, leadership, courage, etc. It was written in 1882 and would become the basis for rethinking global naval strategy in the late Nineteenth and early Twentieth Centuries. About the Battle of Lake Erie he wrote:

"The British ships were fought as resolutely as their antagonists, not being surrendered till they were crippled and helpless . . . (Perry's) two brigs were more than a match for the whole British squadron. In short, our victory was due to our heavy metal. As regards the honor of the affair, in spite of the amount of (American) boasting it has given rise to, I should say it was a battle to be looked upon as in an equally high degree creditable to both sides. . . . Captain Perry showed indomitable pluck and readiness to adapt himself to circumstances; but his claim to fame rests much less on his actual victory than on the way in which he prepared the fleet that was to win it. Here his energy and activity deserve all praise, not only for his success in collecting sailors and vessels and in building the two brigs, but above all for the manner in which he succeeded in getting them out on the lake."

To underscore Roosevelt's praise of the man: Perry was twenty-seven when he arrived to take naval command of Lake Erie and twenty-eight when he won the Battle of Lake Erie.

The consequences of the Battle of Lake Erie were most significant. During the summer of 1813 while the British still had a naval presence on the lake to protect their supply lines, General Henry Procter's army and Tecumseh and his Native American warriors laid siege in May to Fort Meigs, a well designed earthen and timber fortification built on the Maumee Rapids in Ohio under the direction of Eleazer Wood, one of the first graduates from West Point. Despite heavy pounding, the siege failed although many from a Kentucky relief force were killed and captured by the British. Procter and Tecumseh tried again in July but again the fort withstood the attack, so in August they sent some of their force to attack Fort Stephenson on the Sandusky River but this, too, held so they returned to Canada, much to the objection of Tecumseh who urged the British to fight on.

When the British lost control of Lake Erie in September, General Procter knew he had to withdraw from positions he had held but which could no longer be defended without logistical support over the Lake. Thus he abandoned Fort Detroit and even Fort Malden on his own soil and retreated to the interior up the Thames River. Perry repaired his now larger fleet and transported General Harrison's troops to the western end of the Lake where they were joined by a large force from Kentucky and Ohio. Harrison led his army of over 5,000 to reoccupy Fort Detroit, take over the abandoned Fort Malden and pursue General Proctor and Tecumseh. The latter made a stand at Moraviantown. Harrison gave approval to Congressman Richard M. Johnson and his well-trained cavalry of 1,200 horsemen armed with muskets, not sabers, to mount a frontal assault through the woods. The unusual spectacle unnerved the defenders who were caught in a crossfire once the mounts broke through their lines. They surrendered but Tecumseh's warriors vanished once they learned their chief had been killed. Importantly, this was the end of the British-Native American alliance that had been so significant and the end of the British threat to the American Northwestern Territories.

Lake Champlain: 1813

In his definitive book the Naval War of 1812 Theodore

Roosevelt stated what historians have echoed since that book was published 130 years ago about Thomas Macdonough, the U.S. Navy Commodore in charge of Lake Champlain:

"It will always be a source of surprise that the American public should have so glorified Perry's victory over an inferior force, and have paid comparatively little attention to Macdonough's victory, which really was won against decided odds in ships, men and metal. . . . Lake Erie teaches us the advantage of having the odds on our side; Lake Champlain, that, even if they are not, skill can still counteract them."

In the spring the Americans controlled Lake Champlain, the vital, north-south avenue from Canada into the heart of New York. The Richelieu River connected the St. Lawrence River to the Lake and the Hudson River provided water access to the south – to Albany and New York City. Twenty-nine-year-old Lieutenant Thomas Macdonough who had fought in the Barbary War with distinction had superseded the former commander of Lake Champlain, Lt. Sydney Smith, who now reported to him. In June Macdonough sent his naval force consisting of the ***U.S. Sloops Growler*** (11) and ***Eagle*** (11) and six galleys mounting one gun each under Lt. Smith up the Lake to the mouth of the Richelieu/Sorel River to harass the fleet of gunboats the British kept at their fort at Isle-aux-Noix. Unfortunately for Smith, he pursued the gunboats too close to the fort and the wind gave out making it impossible to escape the current of the north-flowing river. After some considerable struggle, the sloops were taken and the naval power balance on this strategically important body of water shifted in favor of the British.

Much like on Lake Erie and Lake Ontario, both nations were building ships as fast as they could to take and more securely hold control of Lake Champlain. As noted earlier, the grand invasion of Canada the Americans planned for the fall of 1813 involved attacking Montreal from the east with an American army from Plattsburg, the town on the western side of Lake

Champlain. That army was to move north up Lake Champlain to the Richelieu River and then up the Saint Lawrence River to Montreal while another American army from Sackets Harbor on Lake Ontario came down the Saint Lawrence to attack Montreal from the west. The campaign failed for a number of reasons. Principal among them was the naval reversal at Isle-aux-Noix at the north end of Lake Champlain enabled the British to block the Richelieu/Sorel River. Instead, the American army under Major General Wade Hampton decided to march west from Plattsburg to the Chateauguay River that provided another route north to Montreal but the British under Lieutenant Charles de Salaberry repulsed him on October 26 at the Battle of the Chateauguay. Meanwhile, the British had also prevented the American attack on Montreal from the west at the Battle of Crysler's Farm. In 1814 it was the British turn to attack the United States.

Lake Champlain: 1814

With the Napoleonic War coming to a close in Europe, seasoned troops were available to dedicate to the North American theater and the Governor General of Canada, Lieutenant General Sir George Prevost was able to assemble an army of 12,000 to go down Lake Champlain, invade New York and take Plattsburg. Aware of the importance of protecting his long supply lines and protecting his flanks, Prevost waited until the British on Lake Champlain had built a fleet superior to that of the Americans. The British squadron under Captain George Downie had recently launched the largest ship on the Lake, almost a blue water frigate, the ***Confiance*** (37) of 1,200 tons that boasted thirty long 24 pounders on the gun deck and a swivel carriage 24 long on the foredeck with six 32 pounder carronades. It even had a furnace for hot shot and was and still is the largest warship ever built on that Lake. At the urging of General Prevost, the ship was rushed into battle not yet fully completed. In addition to the two American sloops taken the year before, renamed the ***Chubb*** and ***Finch***, Downie had the new ***H.M. Brig Linnet*** (16) launched in April and twelve gunboats each armed with cannon.

Macdonough had to fight to get resources and men to build his fleet. Frustrated that Commodore Isaac Chauncey, in charge of the Great Lakes naval forces would not release any to the Lake Champlain effort, Macdonough sent his second in command to visit the Secretary of the Navy and as a result got the famous naval architect Noah Brown back from Chauncey and began building in earnest. The results were the 734 ton ***U.S. Sloop-of-War Saratoga*** (26) armed with eight 24 long cannon, twelve 32 pounder carronades and six 42 pounder carronades; the ***U.S. Brig Eagle*** (20) with eight long cannon and twelve 32 pounder carronades; ***U.S. Schooner Ticonderoga*** (17); the ***U.S. Sloop Preble*** (7); and gunboats each mounting a 24 or 18 pounder long cannon.

A comparison of the two fleets technically would slightly favor the British in terms of tonnage, number of crew and broadside weight although what counted about the latter was the relative strength in long guns (the British) versus the short range carronades (the Americans). The number of vessels was also approximately evenly matched. However, the size of the ***Confiance*** was a distinct advantage for the British.

Macdonough coolly formulated his strategy having weighed all aspects of the situation. He knew his strength was in short guns, and thus close action while his adversary's strength was long guns. By anchoring in Plattsburg's harbor, Cumberland Bay, he forced a close engagement and reduced his exposure to prolonged long gun barrages. And, in the most insightful manner, he knew his ships would probably take a beating from the massive ***Confiance*** so he anchored with spring cables that would allow him to stay in place but turn his ships completely to expose their undamaged gun batteries. He arranged his ships on a north-south axis with one side facing the enemy and the other side protected from the enemy by proximity to the shore and shallow water. Similarly, he anchored the northern-most vessel close to the land so the enemy could not go around his line of battle.

Captain Downie planned his attack on Macdonough for September 10 but had to postpone it for a day because there was no wind. The next morning a gentle breeze blew from the north so he took his entire squadron south, rounded Cumberland Head and sailed into Plattsburg harbor to engage the waiting American fleet. The beginning of the battle was announced when a ball from a British cannon hit the hencoop on the ***Saratoga***'s deck, freeing a cock that alighted and crowed loudly, giving cause for the Americans to rally and let out a cheer. Immediately afterward, Macdonough himself fired the first shot from a 24 pounder long gun that penetrated the hull of on the oncoming ***Confiance*** near its hawse hole, raking the gun deck and killing and wounding several men. But the ***Confiance's*** cool-headed Captain Downie did not return fire until he was ready. On calm water he carefully took aim and then broadsided the ***Saratoga*** with sixteen long 24 pounders each double-shotted. The American ship was so shaken that most of its crew were thrown to the deck. Forty were killed or wounded. Downie was soon killed and Macdonough twice was knocked unconscious, first when hit in the head by a falling spar and then when hit in the face by the flying head of a seaman decapitated by a cannon ball. Battle was intense up and down the line and two ships drifted out of action, the ***H.M.S. Chub*** and the ***U.S.S. Preble***. Macdonough in the ***Saratoga*** bore the brunt of the action. Twice his ship had been set afire by hot shot and gradually all of his engaged guns were silenced. But for his foresight, the battle would have been over. However, he sprung the cables to rotate the ship and brought a complete, undamaged battery into action, as did his other ships. The British tried the same but were unsuccessful. After two and a half hours of battle, the British struck but their gunboats escaped into the Lake. None of the large ships on either side had masts left that could carry canvas and the hulls were cut up and taking on water. The ***Saratoga*** had fifty-five shot holes in its hull while the ***Confiance*** had 105 and the smaller vessels suffered similarly. The Americans lost fifty-eight killed and, depending upon the definition, had up to 140 wounded. It is estimated that the British lost more than sixty killed and suffered up to 300 wounded but the tally is not exactly known because their gunboats scattered at the end of the engagement.

Although British General Prevost had told Captain Downie he would attack Plattsburg as soon as the naval action began in the harbor, he was delayed and had no sooner sent his advance troops forward than he learned of Downie's defeat whereupon he ordered a hasty retreat to Canada. This did not sit well with his men or with his superiors for he subsequently was relieved of command.

That was the last major action on the northern border. Unbeknown to any of them, talks were under way in Belgium that eight weeks later would result in the Treaty of Ghent, signed on Christmas Eve, 1814. The war officially ended when it was ratified and proclaimed on February 17, 1815.

CHAPTER SIX

War on Brown Water

Soon after the War of 1812-1815 started, the main theater of naval activity began moving from the blue waters of the oceans to the brown waters of American bays, sounds, estuaries and rivers. This was not by American choice but dictated by British strategy and might and was made possible by a favorable turn of events in the Napoleonic War. Never fully recovering from their disastrous invasion of Russia in 1812, the French suffered another major defeat in October 1813 at the Battle of Leipzig in Saxony (present day Germany). This forced Napoleon's retreat back to France and his eventual abdication in the spring of 1814. These developments freed up military assets for the British to redeploy to the American theater of war.

In response to the initial success of the American Navy and privateers during 1812, the British Admiralty ordered its frigates not to engage with American frigates on a one-to-one basis and it began to institute more stringent convoy requirements. The British knew from the beginning that the most effective way to deal with the Americans was to bottle up their navy and merchantships by blockading them in port. This would not only eliminate more embarrassing American naval victories but also, more to the point, begin to strangle commerce and the economy and, importantly, cut off funding of the American government that came principally from tariffs on trade. While shipping is still a key part of modern day transportation (a fact not appreciated because most people do not see ships, only trucks, trains and even planes), in the early Nineteenth Century, before roads, canals and railroads appeared on the American landscape, coastal, river and ocean shipping was how goods moved. The British strategy was sound. The problem was in 1812 and for most of 1813 their military assets were dedicated to defeating Napoleon.

Following the October 1813 victory over Napoleon at Leipzig, the British began to divert ships and seasoned troops to establish a stranglehold on America. The growing death grip can be appreciated by looking through the tightening noose of the blockade they began to establish in 1813 and following it to the devastation wrought on brown waters to American seaports and shipping by the summer of 1814. As an instrument of policy, the British did not use the blockade heavy-handedly. They appreciated the enormous American political division over the war and the fact that those who lived in Atlantic coastal states and who favored the war were found in the mid-Atlantic and southern states while the anti-war Federalists were in shipping- and commerce-oriented New England. Thus, in the spring of 1813 when the British first "proclaimed the blockade," it was against the Delaware and Chesapeake Bays.

The "Proclamation of a Blockade" was a recognized legal action that all parties of that time understood. Interestingly, a formal blockade required that the proclaiming party had to have the wherewithal to enforce and maintain it. As the British were able to direct more and more military assets to deal with the Americans, they could and did broaden the blockade up and down the American coast. Later that spring of 1813, they expanded it to major ports in other mid-Atlantic and Southern states and in November of that year, they added the remaining ports in the South and included Long Island Sound in the North. During that same year, the British issued from their main North American naval headquarters in Halifax, Nova Scotia licenses to New England merchants to ship American grain and foodstuffs to General Wellington who was engaged with the French in the Iberian Peninsula. This served two purposes for the British. It fed its army and it supported economically those against the war in America. However, as the war in Europe came to an end in the spring of 1814, the British extended the Proclamation to include New England and the nature of the blockade changed from that of 1813 where limited resources focused on stopping and confiscating shipping in American ports to a much more aggressive war effort in 1814. The noose of the 1813 blockade was very different from the death grip of 1814.

Blockades did not just stop shipping. They required resources to be maintained. This involved obtaining food and supplies for the hundreds or thousands of sailors, marines and stationed troops. Where possible and politic, the British were willing to buy these goods - and on many occasions the commerce-starved Americans were willing sellers. Some even used the guise of a neutral flag to facilitate such trade. In fact, there was so much commerce going on, largely with the enemy, the Madison administration was able to convince Congress to pass an embargo of all American ships in port and all exports in late 1813. This, of course, only brought more economic hardship and further reduced government revenues. It was suicidal and was repealed at Madison's request only four months later.

Later in 1814 the noose tightened as the British presence grew and they began to use force more openly to destroy shipping, seaport towns and facilities. No longer a simple blockade, the war involved forceful occupation, destruction and even plunder. Many communities suffered, but a closer look at three theaters along the Atlantic coast demonstrates the nature of this brown water warfare: Long Island Sound, the eastern coast of Maine and the Chesapeake Bay.

Long Island Sound

The ***U.S. Frigates United States*** and ***Macedonian*** spent the winter of 1812-1813 in New York City undergoing repairs and restocking. They were ready to return to sea by May, 1813 but were blockaded by the British patrolling south of the city at the Sandy Hook entrance, so Captain Stephen Decatur and his squadron consisting of the ***United States***, ***Macedonia*** and the ***U.S. Sloop-of-War Hornet*** sailed north through Hell Gate on the East River to gain access to Long Island Sound and the open ocean. Aside from a bolt of lightning that struck the mainmast of the ***United States*** and rattled its crew, all went well until they reached the eastern end where they encountered a squadron of British ships that had corked up the Sound. So they retreated up the Thames River to New London Harbor on the eastern end of the Connecticut coast. That was the first of June; the frigates would be there until the end of the war - more than a year and a half later. The formal blockade of Long Island Sound would be proclaimed later that year but it was obviously already in effect during the summer of 1813.

The ***H.M.S. Ramillies*** (74) under Captain Thomas Masterman Hardy and the ***H.M. Frigate Orpheus*** (38) under Sir Hugh Pigot patrolled the Sound to make sure the Decatur squadron did not escape. Captain Hardy was a highly respected and seasoned Royal Navy officer of "Kiss me, Hardy" fame. This was the famous command in the 1805 Battle of Trafalgar that Vice Admiral Nelson gave to Captain Hardy as Nelson lay dying on the deck of his flagship the ***H.M.S. Victory*** (100) that Hardy captained.

During the beginning months of patrolling the Sound, Captain Hardy struck a successful balance between civility and hostility to the Americans. However, as time passed and more shipping was captured on the Sound and the Americans became increasingly concerned about raids on their towns, ships and marine facilities, local volunteer militias formed up and defensive plans were made to deal with attacks. The big ships drew too much water to get close to most harbors and towns but their boats, loaded with marines and even cannon could pursue commercial vessels trying to escape into harbors or up rivers or could raid those anchored in the harbors and cut them out or burn them, destroy docks and buildings, pillage for provisions, etc. So local militia, armed with muskets and small field pieces, established watches and used church bells or other signals to assemble defenses quickly. This occurred frequently day and night at all times of the year.

Lacking a naval force to take more aggressive measures, local citizens devised ingenious tactics to rid Long Island Sound of the British menace. This only heightened anxiety aboard the British ships and made the situation even more charged. The ***Eagle*** incident was a prime example of a baited trap. In order to make an attractive quarry for the British to capture, in the spring of 1813 some Americans arranged a cargo of food and provisions, which were much in demand by the British fleet, so they were easily seen on the deck of the merchant schooner ***Eagle***. In truth, below the flour barrels and vegetable crates on the deck was a hold full of explosives and flammables, set to go off once the ***Eagle*** was captured (as it was) and once the American crew jumped ship (as they did) and once the ***Eagle*** was tied up next to the 74-gun ***Ramillies*** (which it was not). Rather, the cautious Hardy instructed the ***Eagle*** be moored next to another captured merchantship. This was an insightful move on his part for the ***Eagle*** did blow but took with it the merchantship and several sailors, not the ***Ramillies***. Thereafter Hardy took further precautions against this sort of attack by no longer allowing American small craft to come alongside his ships as they had done customarily to sell flour, fish, meats, vegetables, etc.

Then there was the attempt to sink the ***Ramillies*** with a version of a submarine designed and used (unsuccessfully) during the Revolutionary War. It reportedly got under the ship three times but was unable to affix the explosive charge. Similarly, what would be called mines today were tried but to no avail. All of this prompted Hardy to drag chains held on either side of his ships from the bow to the stern to check for attached munitions. Faced increasingly with these sorts of annoyances, it was no wonder that Hardy was often found at the mouth of the Sound on Block Island, known to be friendly to the British and a source of fresh water and livestock, or with his friend John Gardiner, who was pro-British and entertained ships' officers at his home on Gardiners Island located between the two eastern forks of Long Island. Finally, when Hardy learned that the Americans planned to attack with a fleet of whaleboats acting as fireboats, he announced that if that happened he would fire every house along the Sound. Nothing happened. But things were getting ugly.

The British demonstrated that they also could play the game of *ruse de guerre*. They would take a captured fishing vessel, load it with Sailors and Marines hidden out of sight, approach a merchantship in an innocent fashion, come alongside and suddenly board and take it. Word soon spread and it became more difficult to repeat this particular *ruse de guerre* on others. Another version, on a grander scale, involved painting the hull and bending old sails on a naval ship to make it look like an old merchantship - an attractive target for a privateer. Once the quarry was lured close enough, the veil would be lifted and tables turned in the flash of a broadside.

One British ship that was part of the Hardy Squadron, the ***H.M. Brig Borer***, engaged in this type of *ruse de guerre* but is better remembered for the "Burning of the Fleet" at Essex, Connecticut in the spring of 1814. Located near the mouth of the

Connecticut River, the town of Essex (formerly named Potopaug) dates back to the Seventeenth Century. At the time of the war, it was an active shipbuilding community and launched many fast privateers. This is probably what attracted the British. In any case, under the cover of darkness on night of April 7, 1814 Captain Richard Coote of the ***H.M. Brig Borer*** led a flotilla of six ship's boats carrying 136 Royal Marines six miles up the Connecticut River and in the early hours of April 8, systematically torched the ships at anchor and on the ways but did not set fire to the town. By sunrise, they were retreating with three ships loaded with captured provisions, including a good deal of rum, but they grounded and all the following day local militia fired on them. Eventually the retreating British torched the ships and returned by their boats alone. Twenty-seven vessels were lost valued at a sum thought to be the single largest commercial loss of the war. Every year the "Burning of the Fleet" is commemorated in Essex.

Later that summer there were more British fireworks when Captain Thomas Masterman Hardy, acting under orders from Rear Admiral George Cockburn to destroy towns along the New England coast, assembled a squadron of five ships including his ***Ramillies*** (74), the ***H.M. Frigate Pactolus*** (44), the ***H.M. Sloops-of-War Dispatch*** (22) and ***Nimrod*** (20) and the ***H.M. Bombship Terror*** off the town of Stonington, Connecticut located a few miles east of New London. Hardy then sent notice to the town that if the town did not surrender, in one hour the fleet would begin to bombard it. The townspeople replied they had no intention of surrendering and sent their women and children away to safety. After three days of impressive bombardment with cannon, mortars and Congreve rockets (as in "rockets' red glare" in the National Anthem), the British withdrew leaving forty homes damaged and four destroyed but no one killed. Every year on the tenth of August the town celebrates the "Battle of Stonington" with parades and ceremonies. Although the attacks on Stonington and Essex are better known today because of their annual commemorations, there were many other seaport towns in New England that the British to one degree or another treated in a similar fashion.

During the spring of 1814 the captains and crews of the blockaded American ***Frigates United States*** and the ***Macedonian*** were redeployed. Meanwhile the ships were moved further up the Thames River for protection and placed "in hulk" (stripped of masts, cannon, etc., but still floating). Captain Decatur and his crew went overland to New York City to man the ***U.S. Frigate President*** and wait for an opportunity to run the blockade to sail with a squadron to the East Indies while Captain Jacob Jones of the ***U.S. Frigate Macedonian*** and his crew went to the Great Lakes to serve with Commodore Chauncey.

The Maine Coast

At the time of the War of 1812-1815, Maine was part of Massachusetts. The northernmost part of eastern Maine jutted north into the eastern territory of British North America that was then called Lower Canada. This knife-like presence of American territory prevented any direct east-west overland route from Halifax (or from St. John on the mainland) to Quebec. If the eastern half of Maine were in the hands of the British, that problem would be eliminated and an ongoing dispute about the common border of that thinly populated area resolved. Moreover, by occupying that half of Maine, the British would be in a better bargaining position in postwar peace negotiations. Accordingly, the British Government ordered the Governor of Nova Scotia, Sir John Sherbrooke, to take the eastern coast of Maine – from Eastport on Moose Island (the easternmost town in the United States) to Castine, on the eastern bank of the Penobscot River that enters the Atlantic halfway down the Maine coast.

The operation began on July 11, 1814 when Captain Thomas Masterman Hardy transported one thousand troops under Lieutenant Colonel Andrew Pilkington from Halifax to Eastport. Faced with an overwhelming force, the eighty-five American Soldiers of Fort Sullivan that defended Eastport surrendered and the British established their eastern beachhead.

The western one followed when Rear Admiral Edward Griffith with a squadron of eight ships ferried 2,500 men under Sir John Sherbrooke to the small port town of Castine on September 1. He then worked his way up the Penobscot River to Bangor and en route encountered the American Captain Charles Morris who burned his ship, the ***U.S. Frigate Adams*** (28), to keep it out of the hands of the British. Subsequently, the British took the coastal port town of Machias, roughly half way between Eastport and Castine. The Massachusetts Militia, occupied with other more pressing problems, decided not to try to retake the coast, especially since it would be virtually impossible without naval support and whatever of that could be mustered would be significantly outgunned by the British fleet in nearby Halifax. So that part of Maine remained in British control until after the war when all original borders were reinstated under terms of the peace treaty.

The Chesapeake Bay

As the war began, the British were fully aware of their strategic vulnerability in Upper Canada – the lands north of New York, Pennsylvania and Ohio. It was a remote wilderness and far from Britain's military strength that was tied down in Europe and landlocked from the Royal Navy. The British decided to take some of the American pressure off of the northern border in 1813 by using the assets it did have available, namely the Royal Navy, to cause the Americans to redirect their military attention. There were two natural targets. The Chesapeake Bay was an active commercial, agricultural and trading area that also offered two important metropolitan targets, Baltimore and Washington, D.C, the Capitol. The other was New Orleans, at the mouth of a river system that was critical to the survival of all of western America. Moreover, the population in the West actively supported the war in Upper Canada by providing troops and supplies. British control of New Orleans would further the existing alliances with Native Americans who provided manpower that the British could not spare from their European wars. As a Southern city, it could also figure into another British strategy to weaken the American South, namely, encourage a slave revolt. Slaves fleeing plantations could be recruited for military service in defending New Orleans, once the city was taken. However, in the end, the British decided the Chesapeake was the greater priority and would have the greatest, most immediate effect on American efforts along the Northern border.

Chesapeake Bay 1813

Thus, in the spring of 1813 Rear Admiral George Cockburn, who was in charge of the Chesapeake blockade and who was acting under orders of Admiral Sir John Borlase Warren, the Commander of the North American Station at Halifax, moved into the Chesapeake and sailed to the northern part of the Bay. There he destroyed a depot at Frenchtown on the Elk River and as he sailed south past where the Susquehanna River empties into the Bay, he was reportedly annoyed when he saw an American flag flying defiantly above a battery at the town of Havre de Grace. Since the town was protected by shallow waters and shoals, Cockburn could not bring his ships to attack it. So under the cover of darkness he sent more than one dozen ship's boats across the shoals to burn and sack the town on May 3, leaving two-thirds of it in ashes. There was no loss of life since the residents had fled. Americans were shocked, in part because they probably were unaware their own countrymen had torched Canadian towns just months before and had forced those residents out empty-handed into the dead of winter. Cockburn continued his path of destruction up the Susquehanna River for a distance, burned buildings and destroyed an important iron works and cannon foundry at Principio.

Admirals Warren and Cockburn then orchestrated an attack at the southern end of the Bay on the Gosport Navy Yard and Marine base in Portsmouth. Blockaded in the Bay, the ***U.S. Frigate Constellation*** had taken safe harbor there. Here the Bay empties into the Atlantic so the ***Constellation*** could quickly run the blockade if propitious circumstances arose. The Navy Yard and Portsmouth were across the Elizabeth River from Norfolk and all three were only accessible through a series of channels that ran through mud flats and past an island where early seamen saw hundreds of cranes (actually they were herons) and named it Craney Island. Preparing for the attack, Brigadier General Robert B. Taylor in charge of the Virginia Militia in the area, blocked off the Elizabeth River and began fortifying Craney Island at the harbor entrance with a fort and redoubts manned by the Militia with field artillery pieces from Portsmouth but also naval guns and a hundred and fifty Navy Sailors and Marines from the ***Constellation***. The British arrived with a force rarely seen at that time: three 74s, one 64, four frigates, a number of troop ships and several lesser vessels. Unable to get past the obstacles placed on the Elizabeth River, in the early morning of June 22 the British sent a force of a couple thousand to attack the island by land and an amphibious force of two thousand including 700 Royal Marines to attack in fifty barges led by the colorful 52-foot ***Centipede*** that mounted a brass cannon in its bow. The defenders did not open fire until the barges were well within range and, even though both sides of the island were attacked in the course of the battle, the defenders held their ground against this vastly superior force. The British retreated after suffering an estimated 200 casualties, half of whom were killed, and losing a number of their barges, three of which sunk in shallow water and ***Constellation*** crewmen recovered. The ***Centipede*** and twenty-two of its crew were also captured. There were no American reported deaths in this successful defensive action.

As if to vent their frustration, on June 26, the British attacked Hampton, a small port town located five miles to the north of Norfolk across the famous Hampton Roadstead (Roads). The defending Militia was overwhelmed and those citizens who remained witnessed every kind of destruction and violence – pillage, rape, murder and the complete destruction of the town. It was all done with impunity, the British later arguing that a corps of Frenchmen – the Chasseurs Britannique, former British prisoners recruited from prison ships and who had a reputation for violent ways - were responsible. The French corps was returned to Halifax and subsequent attacks along the Eastern Shore in August (Kent Island, St. Michaels, Queenstown) proved far less destructive.

Captain Joshua Barney, a colorful American Revolutionary War hero, watched what the British were doing on the Bay in 1813 and offered the U.S. Navy his service and an idea: To build a flotilla of gunboats especially designed for warfare on the Chesapeake with its thousands of miles of coastline, hundreds of estuaries and creeks and, in particular, its shallow waters and fickle winds. He dramatically presented this concept on July 4, 1813. The Navy Secretary Jones accepted it and the following spring the "Chesapeake Flotilla" otherwise known as "Barney's Flotilla" was launched. By September 1813, the bulk of the British fleet withdrew to winter quarters in Bermuda, leaving the Bay in peace but still blockaded.

Chesapeake Bay 1814

During 1813 the Governor-in-Chief of British North America (Canada) asked those in charge of the operations against the Americans, namely Admiral Sir John Borlase Warren in Halifax and General Robert Ross in the Royal Naval Station in Bermuda, to deal with the Americans the same way the Americans had dealt with the British in Canada when they burned York. The highly regarded General Ross arrived in Bermuda with 3400 battle-proven troops from the European campaign in July, 1814 and established their base of operation on Tangier Island - in the middle of the southern part of the Chesapeake Bay.

One of the first naval engagements of the new season occurred on the western shore of the Bay on the first of June when Commodore Joshua Barney's newly launched flotilla of roughly twenty vessels met the ***H.M. Schooner St. Lawrence*** (12) and ship's boats from two British 74s the ***Dragon*** and the ***Albion***. Barney had seven, seventy-five-foot, sloop-rigged boats capable of being rowed, another six measuring fifty feet and an assortment of other vessels, including Barney's flagship, the forty-nine-foot

U.S. Gunboat Scorpion (4). In the Battle of St. Jerome Creek, Barney drove the surprised British back until they reached the safety of their 74s. The Americans then retired to the safety of the Patuxent River. When the British returned, they bottled up the Americans in a tributary feeding the River. With the eventual assistance of troops commanded by officers of the U.S. Army and U.S. Marines, Barney fought his way out in the Battle of St. Leonard's Creek and regained the open water of the main river but, pursued by the British, had to retreat further up the river while the British burned the town of St. Leonard. The Americans retreated up river to Benedict where the British bombarded the town and flotilla for several days. Barney was commanded to take his vessels further up the river to Queen Ann where, if the British pursued, he was instructed to burn his boats. This happened on August 22 in the Battle of Queen Ann.

Although one can question the success of Barney's flotilla, it is credited with two important accomplishments. It delayed the British attack on Washington and Baltimore because the main British invasion route turned out to be the Patuxent River and it was right on Barney's heels as he fought his slow retreat up the river. More specifically, immediately following the destruction of his flotilla, Barney and the Sailors and Marines of his flotilla joined in the defense of Washington at the Battle of Bladensburg on August 24. With two 18 pounder and two 12 pounder naval cannon hastily brought up from the Navy Yard in Washington, they provided the only meaningful resistance in what was otherwise a rout by the British. This became known as the "Bladensburg Races," the counterpart to the rout of British ships in a battle on Lake Ontario in 1813 known as the "Burlington Races." Out of ammunition and vastly outnumbered, the Navy Sailors and Marines fought hand to hand combat and were the last to retreat from the battle. They then went north to defend Baltimore.

General Ross continued to Washington after Bladensburg and, meeting little resistance, set about burning and looting the major public buildings including the Senate and House wings of the Capitol building (the center dome section had yet to be built) the Library of Congress, the Treasury Building, the War Department and the White House. Meanwhile, the retreating Americans torched the Navy Yard and two new ships on the ways there, the ***U.S. Frigate Columbia*** (44) and the ***U.S. Brig Argus*** (18), named after the ship whose impressive record ended a year before. A separate Royal Navy force attacked up the Potomac River, took the rich port town of Alexandria without a fight, and carried off great quantities of warehouse provisions but did not torch the town. A violent storm with torrential rain checked the fire in Washington and, a day after they arrived, the British withdrew and headed to Baltimore where the "Baltimore Defenders" were busy preparing for British land and sea attacks.

Baltimore is well protected from attack from the water by Fort McHenry at the entrance to Baltimore Harbor. The Americans sank a line of merchant vessels to further harbor defenses. The best land route for an army transported by ships to attack the city was through a long peninsula called North Point that extends several miles into the Bay and offers protected harbors for easy disembarkation. The British had 5,000 troops to attack on land and its fleet of ships to attack by sea. Major General Samuel Smith of the Maryland Militia, in overall command of the forces defending Baltimore, sent Brigadier General John Stricker with 2,000 men to fortify, engage and delay the oncoming British five miles from the City and thereby give the defenders more time to prepare. They dug in at a narrow neck of the peninsula while General Ross and 5,000 troops landed at North Point on September 12. In the opening conflict the British suffered a major loss when an American rifleman killed General Ross; this unexpected death of a man who had survived the trials of the Napoleonic War with honors rattled the British command. It was further weakened when it devolved onto a much less competent officer, Col. Arthur Brooke. Nonetheless, the British pressed forward while, as anticipated, the Americans fell back from their defenses at North Point to Hampstead Hill, which was the major defensive line stretching three miles around the eastern side of

Baltimore. U.S. Navy Commodore John Rodgers oversaw its construction; it was much stronger than the British anticipated and had one hundred cannon and ten thousand men under the overall command of U.S. Army Major General Samuel Smith. British attempts to bring naval firepower to bear were successfully frustrated by the guns at Fort McHenry while an attempt to right flank the strong American line had been anticipated and was successfully thwarted. In the early morning hours of September 14, the British viewed further pursuit as hopeless and ordered a retreat back to their ships.

Meanwhile the Royal Navy brought a number of specialized ships to bombard Fort McHenry including the ***Rocket Ship Erebus***, specially designed to launch 32 pound Congreve rockets from a battery below deck through openings on the ship's side. Although highly inaccurate, their visible path, especially at night, coupled with their sound in flight struck terror into those subjected to them. More devastating were the bomb ships that launched fuzzed mortar shells meant to explode in or above defensive fortifications and redoubts. The British ***Bomb Ships Terror***, ***Aetna***, ***Meteor***, ***Volcano*** and ***Devastation*** participated in the twenty-four-hour-long bombardment of Fort McHenry that began the night of September 13. Although the British lobbed an impressive quantity of shells at the Fort from a distance and outside the range of the fort's guns, little damage was done and casualties were minimal. In spite of all the sophisticated hardware brought to the battle, it was a piece of cloth that is remembered today. This very large American flag measuring forty-two feet by thirty feet that Mary Pickersgill and her thirteen-year-old daughter had sewn together won the day when it replaced the fort's riddled battle flag in the morning light of September 14. The Baltimore lawyer and amateur poet Francis Scott Key was on board one of the British ships on a mercy mission under a flag of truce and witnessed the "bombs bursting in air" and the "rockets' red glare" and immortalized this flag when he penned a poem that he put to the music of an old English Bacchanalian song popular at the time in America. Its popularity grew over the subsequent generations and in 1898 the U.S. Navy made it official for ceremonies, a move President Wilson followed in 1916. In 1931 Congress adopted it as the National Anthem.

Gulf Coast: The Conclusion of the War

While the British were conducting their Chesapeake campaign in 1813 and 1814, in the remote hinterland known as the Mississippi Territory (land that is more or less present Mississippi and Alabama), a first-generation Scots-Irish self-made man, Andrew Jackson, was busy becoming a charismatic military leader who soon would assemble a motley mix of Americans of every stripe and color to stop the British cold and win one of the greatest battles of the war. Jackson was born in 1767, taken prisoner at thirteen in the Revolutionary War where he lost his two brothers, was orphaned at fourteen, became a school teacher, lawyer, plantation and slave owner, was elected U.S. Representative and U.S. Senator from the new State of Tennessee, and was promoted to Major General in the Tennessee Militia. Jackson led the military response to the August 30, 1813 attack and slaughter at Fort Mims several miles north of Mobile by a faction of the Creek Indians known as the "Red Sticks." Inspired by calls from the great Native American chief Tecumseh in the Northwest to resist expanding settlements aggressively, the Red Sticks wiped out Fort Mims, slaughtering over 500, scalping half. Jackson mustered an army from the militias in that part of the country and, in what became known as the Creek War, eventually defeated the Red Sticks on March 27, 1814 at the Battle of Horseshoe Bend where over eight hundred Red Stick warriors were killed and more than two hundred wounded. In the resulting Treaty of Fort Jackson, the Creeks turned over most of their territory in a process that would continue for years until most had moved west of the Mississippi.

In mid-September 1814 when the British forces left the Chesapeake Bay following their failure to take Baltimore and subdue Fort McHenry, they sailed to Jamaica to rendezvous with additional troops fresh from the Napoleonic War in Europe for an attack on the American Gulf coast. In preparation for that attack, a British party of one hundred under Major Edward Nicolls had occupied Pensacola in Spanish Florida in August with the tacit approval of the local Spanish authorities. He was to establish a base there to arm and train Native American tribes as potential allies and to gain access to an overland approach to attack New Orleans. The year before, in 1813, Congress declared Mobile, fifty miles to the west, to be American territory and Colonel John Bowyer was sent to build a fort to protect it. Major William Lawrence was in command there in September 1814 with 120 men when the British under Major Nicolls, now based in Pensacola, led a joint land and sea attack on it. In spite of superior force (130 Royal British Marines, 100 Spanish Infantry and 600 Native American Warriors), the British failed to take Fort Bowyer and in the process lost one of its four ships with another severely damaged and suffered ten times the American loss of eight killed and wounded.

Jackson was determined to eliminate British menace in Pensacola so in early November he led over 4,000 troops to the town and demanded the Spanish Governor allow the Americans to replace the British until Spanish troops could protect the town. The Governor refused but surrendered quickly when the Americans began to attack. Meanwhile the British blew their fortifications and embarked on their ships. Then Jackson set out for Mobile, believing the British were going to attack there but received an urgent request to hasten to New Orleans, the real target of the British attack.

General Wilkinson had been in charge of New Orleans but his corrupt and inept ways forced his superiors to move him to the northern theater where his responsibility (and the damage he could do) would be limited. On December 1, Jackson arrived in New Orleans and found the city which had the largest population in the West, 25,000, ill prepared to defend itself and the people with no will to do so. With energy and natural command that he was already known for, the General established land and sea defenses, enlisted militia locally and as far away as Tennessee and welcomed into service backwoodsmen, Native Americans who had been with him, free Blacks and even a powerful group of Baratarian pirates whose base in Grand Terre Island had just been destroyed by the U.S. Navy a couple of months before. He imposed iron discipline both in this motley military assemblage as well as in the city, a task made easy by his dynamic leadership and the evident devotion of his troops as well as by the urgency of imminent attack by a massive, well seasoned and highly professional British force that began to arrive just over a week after Jackson.

With the overland route cut off by General Jackson's attack on Pensacola and the American defenses of Mobile, the British under Vice Admiral Cochrane and Major General Edward Pakenham who was the famous General Wellington's brother-in-law, settled on a sea route to attack New Orleans. By December 13, the main force had arrived off Cat Island, which was a barrier island off the coast about eighty miles from the city. Twenty-nine-year-old U.S. Navy Lieutenant Daniel Patterson, the Master Commandant in command of the New Orleans squadron, anticipated the British arrival and had assembled available vessels to thwart or at least delay the British approach to the city. He placed Lieutenant Thomas ap Catesby Jones[2] in charge of a flotilla of five gunboats (***U.S. Gunboat Numbers 5, 23, 156, 162*** and ***163***), the ***U.S. Schooner Sea Horse*** under Sailing Master William Johnson, and the ***U.S. Sloops-of-War Alligator*** and ***Tickler***. These were manned by a force of 245 men armed with sixteen long guns and fourteen carronades and an assortment of other weapons. Jones positioned his small fleet of gunboats on Lake Borgne to block the entrance to Lake Pontchartrain and the City.

Determined to eliminate this American force, Admiral Cochrane put Commander Nicholas Lockyer of the ***H.M. Brig Sophie*** (18) in command of a fleet of forty-five ship's boats (longboats, barges, and launches) with an assortment of cannon

[2] "ap" is Welsh for "son of."

and 1,200 Royal Navy Sailors and Marines from fourteen ships. They set out the night of December 12 and en route encountered the ***U.S. Schooner Sea Horse***, briefly engaged it but left it under the protection of a shore battery. The Americans subsequently burned the schooner to keep it out of British hands. The British flotilla continued rowing for another day, reaching the Americans on the morning of December 14 but in the process two British boats were cut off and captured by the ***Alligator***.

Then Commander Lockyer organized his boats into three attacking units and took command of the leading one. The Americans anchored their five gunboats and faced their broadsides toward the oncoming enemy. They knew their strength was their cannon range and that, once the British closed, they would be greatly outnumbered and even though they had hung their boarding nets, it would be only a matter of time before a force of 1,200 would overrun the less than 130 on the gunboats. Such was the case and Lockyer expedited the process by going after the American flagship, Lieutenant Jones' ***U.S. Gunboat Number 156*** armed with a long 24 pounder and four 12 pounder carronades. After desperate hand-to-hand fighting during which both Jones and Lockyer were seriously wounded, the British took the vessel and then turned its guns against the remaining four American gunboats. In five minutes, the fight was over. The ***U.S. Sloop-of-War Tickler*** remained out of the action, as ordered by Jones, but the skipper scuttled it to keep it out of the hands of the British. The Americans lost six killed and thirty-five wounded and eighty-six captured as opposed to the British loss of seventeen killed and seventy-seven wounded.

The way was clear to mount the attack on New Orleans. British Major General John Keane established a garrison on Pea Island that was about thirty miles from the city and landed many of the eight thousand troops that came on the first wave of British transports. Additional troops would arrive from Europe later. News of the defeat on Lake Borgne caused panic in New Orleans prompting General Jackson to tighten his grip further by declaring martial law. Nine days later, on December 23, General Keane initiated the attack marching 1,800 of his men north along the east bank of the Mississippi and camped nine miles south of the city. Had he continued, the outcome would have been different for no defenses would have blocked him from the city, but he camped at Villere's Plantation to await reinforcements before proceeding.

Having learned about the British movement, Jackson vowed no British Soldier would sleep on American soil that night and hastened around two thousand troops to the British camp. The U.S. Navy initiated the surprise attack; the ***U.S. Sloops-of-War Louisiana*** (16 - most of which were 24 pounders) under Lt. Charles C. B. Thompson and ***Carolina*** (14) under Lt. John D. Henley opened up a barrage on the camp in the early evening. Then Jackson's troops attacked from different quarters. In the darkness, chaos and confusion, both sides suffered. The British lost forty-six killed and over 230 wounded or missing while Jackson lost twenty-four killed and about 190 wounded or missing.

Jackson fell back to the Rodriguez Canal, a natural line of defense about four miles south of the city, and began to fortify it. Each hour the British delayed their advance Jackson used to strengthen his defenses. General Keane and his fellow officers had high expectations that their battle-hardened troops fresh from the Napoleonic War would easily deal with the poorly trained local militia and anything else the Americans might throw their way so they were doubly surprised by the effective attack. Suddenly more cautious and with a debate raging within their camp between the Army and the Navy as how to proceed, the British stayed encamped.

The American earthen fortifications ran along the north side of the canal from the Mississippi River in the west to a swamp in the east. To protect the Mississippi River flank, Jackson had placed a few hundred men with cannon on the west bank of the river. Both sides continued to strengthen their positions with artillery, the Americans bringing some of their naval guns while the ***Louisiana*** and ***Carolina*** continued to bombard the British from the river. To put an end to this, the British set up a furnace for hot shot and returned fire, successfully torching the ***Carolina*** and forcing the crew of the ***Louisiana*** to tow it out of range.

On the 28th the British sent out a large reconnaissance party and on New Year's Day, the British initiated an artillery dual that lasted three hours until they ran out of ammunition or their guns dismounted. The two sides suffered about 100 casualties, mostly British. Rather than launching an attack at that point, General Pakenham, who had come to the front to take command, decided to wait for the full complement of his over 7,000 troops to join him. He was ready one week later and launched a two-pronged attack the morning of January 8, 1815. The British plan called for Colonel William Thornton to lead 600 men across the Mississippi under the cover of darkness to take the American position on the west bank and turn its guns against the Americans' main line of defense on the east side of the river. Then General Pakenham was to throw his main force of over 5,000 against Jackson's defenses at daybreak. But things did not go as planned. Thornton was delayed until daylight but nonetheless did successfully take the west bank only to be ordered back across the river because the main thrust was delayed. When it was launched the British had the cover of an unexpected thick ground fog, but just as they approached the American defenses, the fog suddenly lifted leaving the troops in full view. Cannon with grape shot and canisters, rifles and muskets rained devastating sheets of lead on the advancing troops. General Packenham bravely led his troops riding back and forth urging them on. He had a horse shot out from under him, mounted another but was killed by a cannon ball. Command fell to Major General John Lambert who called off the attack and asked for a ceasefire to remove the wounded and bury the dead. Jackson agreed. The break gave Lambert time to reflect on the hopelessness of his situation and the extraordinary cost in life were he to resume the battle so he did not, in spite of urging by Admiral Cochrane to do so. The Admiral was still hopeful that his fleet could sail up the Mississippi, pass the American defensive Fort Philip some sixty miles south of the city and support the army in its attack. Fort Philip successfully blocked the river in spite of ten days of continued heavy bombardment. Conceding defeat, the British embarked and sailed east to attack Mobile.

The whole New Orleans campaign between December 23 and January 8 cost the British nearly 2,500 men, twenty percent of whom were captured. The Americans suffered a loss of only 350, including fifty killed and 200 wounded. It was a great defeat for the British Army and, conversely, many viewed it as the greatest American victory of the War of 1812-1815.

A British force of 1,400 men under General Lambert and a naval squadron led by the ***H.M.S. Vengeur*** (74) under Captain Tristram R. Ricketts sailed to attack Mobile. On February 7 it arrived off Fort Bowyer that protected the entrance to Mobile Bay. Over the next five days, the British reconnoitered, landed a force to cut off possible reinforcements reaching the fort from the landward side and began building siege batteries, bringing naval guns onshore. All the while the 375 Americans in the fort continued to fire on the British when possible. When the British battery was in place, it announced its presence with a barrage and Captain William Lawrence, commander of the Americans surrendered in view of the overwhelming force. Although an easy victory - especially compared to hard fought battle at New Orleans - it was hollow for word arrived of the Treaty of Ghent. The British never got to Mobile but embarked on their ships and left. The war on brown water was over.

CHAPTER SEVEN

Epilogue

Immediately after the War of 1812-1815, the U.S. Navy returned to the Barbary Coast to suppress piratical activity that had reemerged following the First Barbary War in 1801-1805. A New York squadron of ships under Stephen Decatur consisting of three heavy frigates and a half dozen other ships departed on May 20, 1815 and, following the capture of his warships, the Dey of Algiers capitulated and signed a peace treaty on July 3. The matter was resolved with such dispatch, that a second squadron that sailed from Boston under William Bainbridge missed the action.

In April 1816, Congress authorized an expansion of the Navy, calling for "nine ships to rate not less than 74 guns each." This was a massive undertaking and led to the construction of the ***U.S.S. Delaware*** and its largest ship, the ***U.S.S. Pennsylvania***, a 120-gun ship that was actually pierced for 136 guns. But these ships-of-the-line served little purpose following the 1815 Treaty of Vienna that ended the Napoleonic War and ushered in the era of "Pax Britannia."

With the return of peace in the "era of good feeling" after the war, the Navy focused on protecting commerce and suppressing pirates who flourished in the many bays, estuaries and rivers of the islands in the Caribbean. By 1830 the problem had largely been eliminated. Slave trade was declared to be piracy in 1819 and those involved were subject to the death penalty. The Navy's African Slave Trade Patrol monitored the West African coast, the Caribbean and the Atlantic shores of South America for the four decades prior to the Civil War. Over these years, many famous frigates saw this duty, including the ***United States*** and the ***Constellation***, extensively rebuilt in 1854.

In 1836 Congress authorized an ambitious exploration mission formally known as the United States Exploring Expedition but referred to as the "U.S. Ex. Ex." or as the "Wilkes Expedition," when command of it devolved from U.S. Navy Commodore Thomas ap Catesby Jones to U.S. Navy Lt. Charles Wilkes. Only the Navy had the ships and ability to execute the Expedition so it sent six ships with cartographers, scientists, botanists, surveyors and artists to explore the waters of Antarctica and the South Pacific, chart the west coast of the Western Hemisphere and collect thousands of plant and animal specimens during the four-year expedition from 1838-1842. It contributed greatly to Nineteenth Century science and knowledge but did involve loss of life and two ships, including the rebuilt ***U.S. Sloop-of-War Peacock*** (10) that was lost on a bar in the Columbia River.

In 1836 the Republic of Texas declared its independence from Mexico but Mexico did not recognize it. This destabilized the vast Mexican territory north of the Rio Grande, an area that includes California and the present-day American Southwest. Americans were concerned that a European power like Russia or the United Kingdom might lay claim to parts of it. In 1842 the Commander of the Navy's Pacific Squadron, Thomas ap Catesby Jones, who was captured at New Orleans by the British and ever wary of them since, heard rumors about British intentions on California and, believing that the United States had already declared war on Mexico, took his squadron, led by his flagship, the ***U.S. Frigate United States,*** to Monterey and laid claim to California. He surrendered it upon learning war had not been declared.

Things became more unsettled in 1845 when the United States admitted Texas into the Union. During the resulting 1846-1848 Mexican War, the U.S. Navy's Pacific Squadron seized the Mexican ports of San Diego, Monterey and San Francisco. On the Gulf coast, the Navy transported Army troops and landed Marines at Veracruz who opened the way to the "Halls of Montezuma" at Chapultepec and victory.

As the result of history, tradition and happenstance, the U.S. Navy was predominantly Northern in makeup and orientation when the Civil War began in 1861 and therefore lost few officers and men to the Confederate Navy. The Union Navy played an important role in defeating the Confederacy through effective blockades of Southern ports and by providing supplies and amphibious support for the Union Army. Its gunboats attacked Confederate strongholds on inland rivers and bays. Moreover its presence effectively kept foreign powers that were commercially sympathetic to the South from influencing the outcome of the war. Confederate blockade-runners did some damage to Northern shipping, however the ***U.S.S. Kearsarge*** and other ships eventually brought them to heel.

Although the Navy had fallen behind a number of European countries in technological advances, the urgency of the Civil War brought it back up to speed not only in ironclads such as the ***U.S.S. New Ironsides,*** but also in design advances as evidenced in the ***U.S.S. Monitor*** and the greater use of screw propulsion for is warships. By the end of the Civil War, the Navy had almost 700 ships including about sixty ***Monitor***-type vessels and 51,500 officers and men. But, as a war-weary people turned their attention to Westward expansion, transcontinental railroads and industrialization and as there were no foreign threats, the Navy shrank to forty-eight ships and 6,000 men by 1880.

Meanwhile the Revenue Cutter Service continued to regulate maritime commerce activities. In 1876 it established the School of Instruction near New Bedford, Massachusetts. Four decades later the School became the Coast Guard Academy when several services that had existed independently (the Revenue Cutter Service, the Lighthouse Service, the Steamboat Inspection Service, the Bureau of Navigation, and the Lifesaving Service) were merged into a new organization, the United States Coast Guard. The Academy is now located at New London, Connecticut. (The Navy had established its Academy at Annapolis, Maryland in 1845.)

The fact that the Navy was shrinking in size and becoming increasingly obsolete was highlighted in 1873 when a Spanish ironclad visited New York City and the Navy (and more importantly, the public) realized that the Navy had no ship to match it. This set several things in motion that brought considerable change over the next decade and led to the "New Navy." One of the first was the design and construction of the ***U.S.S. Wampanoag***, a four-stack, lean, muscle machine that set speed records and impressed European naval designers but had no future because its narrow hull, full of machinery, provided neither stability nor fuel capacity for range.

However, things were stirring on other fronts. In 1882 young Theodore Roosevelt published The Naval War of 1812, an exhaustive analysis of the important elements of naval warfare: strategy, tactics, manpower training, leadership and experience, ship design and construction, etc. Coincidental with this, a naval review for the Secretary of the Navy concluded in 1882 that Spain was not alone in being able to contest American naval power. Other European and even some South American powers also could. As a result, in 1883 Congress authorized construction of the "ABCD Ships." These included three technologically advanced protected cruisers (***U.S.S. Atlanta, Boston*** and ***Chicago***) and a dispatch vessel (***U.S.S. Detroit***) that were known as the "Flying White Squadron" because of their hull color. They proved successful and other ships followed including the first battleships, the ***U.S.S. Texas*** (ordered in 1889) and the ***U.S.S. Maine***. The "New Navy" was underway.

The American Navy and those in Europe were greatly influenced by the 1890 publication of The Influence of Sea Power upon History 1660 - 1783 by the U.S. Navy professor and historian and President of the newly established Naval War College in Newport, Rhode Island, Alfred Thayer Mahan. The importance of control of the sea lanes registered with the American public and government at a time when "Manifest Destiny" was spilling beyond American borders into the Caribbean and Pacific and as more battleships were added to the Navy's fleet in the 1890s.

Thus when war broke out with Spain in 1898, the Navy, under Secretary of the Navy Theodore Roosevelt, played a decisive role in taking the Spanish possessions of Cuba in the Battle of Santiago de Cuba and the Philippines in the Battle of Manila Bay. The latter represented a daring undertaking thousands of miles away from support facilities and influenced American strategic thinking when Roosevelt became President in 1900 and introduced his foreign policy - "Speak softly and carry a big stick." The "Big Stick" was the Navy and he made it bigger by adding more capital ships. In 1907 he introduced America to the world as a rising naval power by sending the Great White Fleet of sixteen capital ships and escorts under the flagship ***U.S.S. Connecticut*** on a fifteen-month circumnavigation of the globe. He also used it actively to intervene in a number of Caribbean and Central American countries and to protect the new Panama Canal from the Navy base at Guantanamo Bay, Cuba.

When the first great European war since the Napoleonic War broke out in 1914, the United States found itself in the same position it was in a century before, namely, trying to be neutral among the belligerents. It was able to stay out of the conflict for three years but unrestricted German submarine warfare led Congress, after months of debate, to pass the Naval Act of 1916 that authorized a large expansion of the Navy. This included ten new battleships, six battle cruisers, ten scout cruisers, fifty destroyers (a number later increased significantly) and sixty-seven submarines. Fortunately the Navy had experience with submarines. It commissioned its first in 1901 and named it after its inventor, the ***U.S.S. Holland***.

America formally entered WWI in April 1917, only months after the Naval Act was passed and before any of those ships were ready for action. So during the twenty months before the war ended in 1918, the Navy focused on convoy duty, moving troops and materiel across the Atlantic and in the Mediterranean but it also sent Marines into action in France and capital ships to assist the British Grand Fleet at its main naval base at Scapa Flow in the Orkney Islands of Scotland. Following the collapse of Germany's ally, the Ottoman Empire (Turkey), at the end of the war, the Navy sent a squadron including the ***U.S.S. Arizona*** to Istanbul to bring stability and protection to an area threatened by the neighboring Soviet Union that emerged following the Russian Revolution in 1917.

At the end of WWI, the Navy was the largest in the world in terms of personnel – nearly half a million. These included African Americans and Yeomen (F) who were the first non-nurse women enlisted in American armed services. Exhaustion from the unprecedented devastation and cost of the war led to the Washington Naval Agreement, a 1922 international treaty to limit navies to ratios of their existing strengths where the United States Navy was formally recognized as the only peer of the Royal Navy. Naval tonnage for both nations was limited to 525,000 and this focused American attention over the next decade on how to best allocate this tonnage among its capital ships. The U.S. Navy chose to put some of it into naval aviation. The first carrier, the ***U.S.S. Langley (CV 1),*** was followed by two others built on the hulls of converted battle cruisers, the legendary ***U.S.S. Lexington (CV 2)*** and ***U.S.S. Saratoga (CV 3).***

The world was changing rapidly in the 1930s and, with the help of Assistant Secretary of the Navy turned President, Franklin D. Roosevelt, Congress authorized in mid-1940 the expansion of the Navy's fleet to 200 ships. In October 1941, two months before Pearl Harbor, a German submarine sank the first American warship, the ***U.S.S. Reuben James.*** This was a destroyer escort named after a U.S. Navy Sailor who nobly took the blow of a samovar to protect his fallen commander, Stephen Decatur, in the First Barbary War and made famous in the song "The Sinking of the Reuben James" by Woody Guthrie.

Japan launched WWII for Americans on December 7, 1941 with attacks on Pearl Harbor and other parts of the Pacific. The Americans concentrated on "Europe first" so the Pacific war was largely defensive initially and focused on convoy protection, anti-submarine warfare, commerce raiding and amphibious support but was highlighted by the Doolittle Raid on Tokyo off the ***U.S.S. Hornet*** and the Battles of the Coral Sea and Midway in 1942. That year the Pacific counter-attack began and led up to the largest aircraft carrier engagement ever, the Battle of the Philippine Sea and the Battle of Leyte Gulf – one of the largest naval battles in history. Iwo Jima led to the eighty-two-day Battle for Okinawa, the largest sea and land battle and one of the bloodiest of the war. The Japanese surrendered on board the ***U.S.S. Missouri*** following the use of atomic bombs. At that time there were 1,200 ships and nearly 3.4 million men and women in the U.S. Navy.

The dramatic downsizing to 300 ships after the war was short-lived as the Cold War began. In the 1950-1953 Korean Conflict the Navy played an important role in the large and risky Inchon Invasion that effectively drove the invading North Koreans back over the border. In the 1950s Admirals like Hyman G. Rickover insured continuing future roles for the Navy with the introduction of nuclear power for ships and submarines, ICBMs and rockets and jets for carriers.

The Navy engaged in Viet Nam (1955-1975) with its blue water carriers and its brown water gunboats. But, again, time was leaving its mark on the size and quality of the fleet that had fallen to just over 200 surface ships and about 100 submarines. Concerned that it was no longer a match for its principal adversary, the Soviet Union, President Reagan set out to build the fleet up to 600. This goal was basically reached in 1988 and was not just quantity but quality, leading the way to super-carriers of the ***Nimitz*** class and nuclear submarines of the ***Ohio*** class. The collapse of the Soviet Union in 1991 was in part due to its inability to maintain this race.

The Navy, Marine Corps and Coast Guard showed American presence in Lebanon (1982-1984) and in Desert Shield (1990) and Desert Storm (1991) of the First Gulf War, the Iraq War (2003-2011) and the ongoing Afghanistan War that began in 2001.

This book began with the opening passages of a statement by Secretary of the Navy Ray Mabus:

"The United States is a maritime nation. This has been a fact throughout our history and remains very much the case today. The oceans connect us to the world, and they sustain our trade and economy. For the past two hundred years, the world's oceans have also witnessed the presence and the growth of the United States Navy and Marine Corps. On the waves, we have become what we are and will remain: the most formidable expeditionary fighting force the world has ever known."

The Secretary went on to conclude:

"This is a journey that began in earnest during the War of 1812, the first true global conflict of our still young and expanding nation. Two hundred years hence on the Quadricentennial of the War of 1812, whatever unknown seas this still young and expanding nation will have sailed, our maritime services will still recognize their voyage began, in earnest, in the War of 1812."

THE END

GLOSSARY OF NAUTICAL TERMS USED IN THIS BOOK

(Italicized Words in descriptions are Defined Words)

Beat to Windward: To Tack in a *Weatherly* direction – into the direction from which the wind is coming.

Bend On: To fasten or attach a sail.

Bow Sprit: A strong spar projecting out from the bow to which headstays are fastened to support the mast and carry foresails.

Brig: A ship with two masts (fore and main), both rigged with square sails.

Brig Sloop: A warship with two masts, rigged as a *brig*. A *sloop-of-war* had three masts.

Brigantine: A ship with two masts where the first mast (the foremast) is rigged with square sails and the aft mast (the mainmast) is rigged with *fore-and-aft* gaff mainsail with one or more square sails above it. When the main mast is rigged with only *fore-and-aft* sails, it was known as a *hermaphrodite brig*.

Broad Pennant: A swallow-tailed tapering naval flag that, when flown, indicates the presence on board of an officer of the rank of commodore or a captain serving in a designated commodore command billet. It is called a "broad" pennant because its dimensions are roughly 2:3.

Broadside: One side of a ship. Also used to describe cannon fire from one side of a ship.

Broadside Weight: The total weight of the projectiles (cannon balls, grape shot, bar shot, etc.) fired from one side (*broadside*) of a ship or a group of ships.

Cannon: Naval cannon in the late Eighteenth and early Nineteenth Centuries were all muzzle loading. They were categorized by the weight of the ball they fired, as in an "18 pounder" or a "24 pounder." Naval guns ranged from 6, 9, 12 to 18, 24 and 32 pounders. In this era, there were long guns and short-barreled *Carronades*. Long guns had greater range and accuracy, effective up to 1200 yards. The weight and dimensions of long guns most often seen in this book were approximately as follows:

18 Pounder: Weight: two tons (with carriage); barrel length: ~ 8'; bore: ~ 5"

24 Pounder: Weight: three tons (with carriage); barrel length: 8' - 10'; bore: ~5½"

Cannon become more effective - more powerful - the more tightly the ball fits into the bore since less exploding gas escapes past the ball. The difference between the diameter of the bore and the diameter of the ball is known as "windage." The smaller the windage, the greater is the ratio of the ball/bore diameters. As cannon making improved in this era of naval warfare, this ratio increased from 20/21 to 24/25 in long guns and reached 34/35 in *Carronades* because the barrel was shorter and could be bored more accurately. This reduction in windage in *Carronades* made them very powerful, short-range weapons.

Carronade: A relatively light cannon with a short barrel that was used for close range engagements, under 400 yards. Most of the Carronades on ships in this book fired a 32 pound ball or shot. A heavier model fired a 42-pound ball or shot. The cannon took its name from the Carron Foundry in Scotland where it was developed. The Carronade's windage (see *Cannon*) reduction not only increased its power but also significantly reduced the amount of powder it used. The Carronade had other design improvements as well. Its greatly reduced weight (a third of the weight of an equivalent *long gun*) meant it could be carried safely on upper decks, bringing much more firepower to a ship. Also, by replacing the trunnions (the axle that supports the cannon barrel on the gun carriage) with a bolt underneath the barrel that connected the gun to its mounting, the width of the carriage was greatly reduced (basically the carriage was eliminated) and this increased the width of the angle of fire out the *gun port* and made the weapon much more versatile.

32 Pound Carronade: Weight: one ton; barrel length: 4'; bore: ~ 6"

Crossing the "T": A tactic in which a warship crosses in front of an enemy ship, in order to bring all its *broadside* guns to bear while receiving fire from only the forward guns of the enemy ship.

Cut Out: To capture or take a vessel from the protection of an enemy convoy or harbor.

Double Shotted: The condition of a *cannon* when loaded with two projectiles (cannon balls, grape shot canister, etc.)

Fighting Sail: A sailing condition going into combat in which the lower sails are hauled up or furled to reduce the risk of fire from cannon activity on the gun deck and to improve visibility for navigation and combat.

Fighting Tops: On early Nineteenth Century *square rigged* ships platforms known as "tops" were mounted where the top of a lower mast overlapped the bottom of the mast above it. The principal function of these "tops" was to provide *standing rigging* for and access to the upper masts. On warships these platforms were known as "fighting tops" because they provided an excellent vantage point and "commanding heights" for marines armed with muskets and small caliber cannon to fire down on the deck of an adversary engaged at close range. Conversely, these "fighting tops" were dangerous places to be for they afforded the marines little or no protection from enemy cannon and small arms fire.

Fore and Aft Rigged: A way in which a ship is rigged wherein the *luff* of the principal sails are *bent on* (attached to) the masts. This is in contrast to *square rigged* where the sails are suspended across the masts on *yards*. Foresails like *jibs* and *staysails* were common to both types of rig and most *square rigged* vessels of the era had at least one *fore and aft* sail mounted on the aft-most mast, known as a Spanker. Similarly, many *fore and aft* rigged ships carried one or more *square rigged* sails as seen in *topsail schooners*.

Frigate: A warship with three masts and two decks: A lower deck that runs from the bow to the stern, the gun deck, and an upper, partially open spar deck. *Cannon* were carried on both decks with the heavier guns below.

Gun Port: The opening in a side of a ship through which a *cannon* can be fired.

Hawse Hole: An opening high on either side of the bow cut through the hause timbers that reinforce the opening and through which a hauser (or large rope) connected to the anchor/anchor chain passes.

Hermaphrodite Brig: See *brigantine.*

Impress: To take a sailor and "press" or force him into involuntary service. The act is called impressment.

In Ordinary: The phrase describing a naval vessel out of service for repair or maintenance. ("In reserve" or "mothballed" are the modern equivalents.)

Jib: A triangular headsail fastened to a headstay above or forward of the bow.

Jib Boom: A removable *spar* fastened to the bowsprit used for mounting one or more *jibs* forward over the bow.

Jibe: To change *tacks* by steering away from the wind so that the *leach* of the sail swings across the eye of the wind.

Leech: The trailing edge of a *fore and aft* sail.

Lee: The direction on board ship to which the wind is blowing. It also refers to that side of the ship as in the "lee side."

Long Gun: A *cannon* with a long barrel as opposed to a short-barreled *carronade.* Generally, the longer the barrel, the greater the accuracy and projectile speed resulting from more efficient and longer use of gas expansion from the explosion in the barrel.

Long Tom: A naval long gun with extra barrel length for greater accuracy.

Luff: The forward edge of a triangular sail.

Mast: A vertical *spar* (timber) on a sailing vessel used to support the sails.

Pistol-shot Range: A very rough measure of distance, about twenty to thirty yards. It was the preferred range for close action since at that distance cannon balls had the power to dismast and penetrate the enemy's hull while the ships were far enough apart that boarding was not possible and there was no possibility of fire in the enemy ship spreading to your own.

Prize Crew: Officers and men put on board a captured ship (prize of war) to take command of it.

Rake: (Verb) 1. To rake is to fire projectiles through a hull lengthwise from bow to stern or *vice-versa*. Since gun decks were largely open in wooden ships, gunners were exposed and very vulnerable to this type of gunfire and, since there were very few, if any, *cannon* facing forward through the bow or aft through the stern, a ship being raked was largely defenseless; (Noun) 2. The angle the *mast* makes with the deck off the perpendicular. Raked masts are angled back toward the stern.

Ratlines: Horizontal lines, usually made of rope, affixed to *shrouds* so as to form a rope ladder that provided access to upper masts and sails.

Rising Weather: The condition at sea when a storm is in the offing.

Schooner: A ship with two or more *masts* that are *fore and aft* rigged.

Scow: A flat-bottom barge with a raked transom at both ends, designed for sailing or rowing in shallow waters.

Seacock: A valve on the hull of a ship or boat that, when open, permits water to flow into or out of the vessel. Opening a seacock was one of the main ways to scuttle a ship to avoid its capture by the enemy.

Ship-of-the-line: More fully stated: Ship-of-the-line-of-battle. These were the largest warships of the time designed to participate in the heaviest engagements, the "line of battle" in which enemy fleets approached each other in single line formations. Over time the phrase was shortened to "battleship."

Shroud: A rope that is part of the *standing rigging* that connects from the top of a *mast* to the side of the vessel to hold the mast in place. Horizontal *ratlines* were often affixed to them to provide ladder access to upper masts and sails.

Slip a Blockade: To successfully evade a blockade.

Sloop-of-War: A warship with three *masts* and a single deck for *cannon* running from the bow to the stern. These were smaller than *frigates*, which also had three *masts* but had two decks for *cannon*: the lower gun deck and the upper spar deck.

Spar: The general term for any of the above-deck timbers to which sails are *bent* (attached), such as the *masts*, booms, gaffs, *yards* and sprits.

Square Rigged: A way in which a ship is rigged wherein four-sided sails are suspended from the middle on yards fastened to the *mast*. All of the early Nineteenth Century *frigates* and *ships-of-the-line* were square rigged.

Square Sail: A four-sided sail *bent on* a *yard* fastened to the *mast*.

Standing Rigging: Permanent rigging on a ship that remains (stands) in place verses "running rigging" used to work the sails and yards.

Stay: A stout rope running fore and aft used to hold a *mast* in place.

Staysail: Usually a triangular sail whose *luff* is attached to a stay.

Tack: (Verb) 1. To turn across the eye of the wind in order to fill the sails on the opposite side and make good a *weather* course; 2. (Noun) The heading of a vessel when sailing close-hauled relative to the wind; one of a series of straight runs that make up the zigzag course of a ship proceeding to windward.

Three-decker: A warship with *cannon* on three decks. These were large ships and were rated *ships-of-the-line*, meaning they were designed to participate in the heaviest engagements, the "line of battle" in which the two adversaries approached each other in single line formations.

Topmast: The *mast* mounted above the lower or mainmast. Topgallant mast would be above the topmast and the royal mast above that.

Topsail Schooner: A *fore and aft* rigged vessel with two or more *masts* with one or more square sails on one or more *masts*.

Two-decker: A warship with *cannon* on two gun decks running from the bow to the stern usually with a partially open spar deck above. These were large ships and were rated *ships-of-the-line*, meaning they were designed to participate in the heaviest engagements, the "line of battle" in which the two adversaries approached each other in single line formations. (See *Warship Ratings* and *Ship-of-the Line.*)

Warship Ratings in the Royal Navy: A system used from the Seventeenth Century to the mid-Nineteenth Century by the Royal Navy to categorize ships initially by the complement of men in the crew but later by the number of carriage-mounted *cannon*.

A first-, second- or third-rate ship was regarded as a *ship-of-the-line* and the first and second rates were three-deckers, that is, they had three continuous decks of guns. Third-rate ships were *two-deckers* and carried sixty-four to seventy-four guns.

Fourth-, fifth- and sixth-rate ships carried fewer guns and their categories often blurred over the years but fifth-rate ships performed the role of *frigates* while sixth-rate could take on no more than convoy duty.

Ways: The construction floor and launching facility where a ship is built usually consisting of two parallel inclined rails leading into the water.

Wear: To turn by hauling about to the opposite *tack* by *jibing.*

Weather: (Noun) 1. The direction from which the wind is blowing; (Verb) 2. To gain the advantage on another sailing vessel by working to weather – by sailing closer to the wind or getting further to the weather.

Weather Gauge (or Gage): A favorable position offering greater maneuverability where a sailing vessel is up-wind (or to the weather) from another sailing vessel that is down-wind (or to the lee). In a sailing ship it is much easier for the former to approach the latter than *vice versa.*

Windward: The direction on board ship from which the wind is blowing. It also refers to that side of the ship as in the "weather side."

Yard: A timber in the rigging of sailing ships to which a square sail, lateen sail or lug sail is *bent.* In American, British and French warships of the early Nineteenth Century, yards were almost always horizontal but in the lateen-rigged Mediterranean ships they were angled.

ACKNOWLEDGMENTS

This book grew out of a video documentary series, the Naval War of 1812 Illustrated, produced by the American Society of Marine Artists (ASMA), the nation's oldest and largest not-for-profit association dedicated to marine art and history (www.americansocietyofmarineartists.com). The seven-part video was created on the occasion of the Bicentennial of the War of 1812-1815. It is free for all and can be found at: www.naval-war-of-1812-illustrated.org.

Many people and institutions contributed generously in various ways to making the video. Sixty museums, historical societies and other institutions in France, the United Kingdom, Canada and the United States, including the museums of the U.S. Navy, Marine Corps and Coast Guard provided images of works in their permanent collections to illustrate the video story line. Additional artwork came from fifty members of ASMA and images of ship models were provided by members of the Nautical Research Guild, one of the nation's most prestigious organizations of model makers. A core group from ASMA helped me drive this three-year effort and should be mentioned by name: Mary "Mimi" B. Merton, Associate Producer; Michael J. Killelea, Design and Art Director; Del-Bourree Bach, Narrator; and Ann H. Mohnkern, J.D. (Retired), Rights Manager.

This book is a story, not an historical treatise, but it is based on history as obtained from countless books, articles and documents written about this period in America, Canada and Europe. In addition, a number of historians have assisted directly. These include: William S. Dudley, Ph.D., Former Director of Naval History for the United States Navy, who also generously contributed the **Foreword** to this book; Donald R. Hickey, Ph.D., Professor at Wayne State College and author of seven books and nearly a hundred articles about the War of 1812; Paul F. Johnston, Ph.D., Curator of Maritime History at the Smithsonian Institution; Lt. Col. Robert J. Sullivan (USMC, Retired), Head of Curatorial Services, National Museum of the Marine Corps; Edward M. Furgol, Ph.D., Director of the National Museum of the United States Navy; James W. Cheevers, Associate Director and Senior Curator and Grant Walker, Education Specialist at the United States Naval Academy Museum; William H. Thiesen, Ph.D., Historian, Atlantic Area, United States Coast Guard; Linda Ferber, Ph.D. Senior Historian, New York Historical Society; Christine F. Hughes, Historian, U.S. Naval History and Heritage Command; Patrick Kavanagh who has researched events of the war in Buffalo, New York; and, Christopher Golding and Joshua Wolf, both doctoral candidates at Temple University whose dissertations deal with naval activities of the war and who helped with early drafts of the narrative.

I am particularly indebted to Mimi Merton not only for her extraordinary organizational ability in managing the hundreds of images and attendant credit information in the video but also for her perseverance, patience and very significant editorial skills in helping translate the video narrative into this book. Also I must note that a friend of many years, Martha Mast Watts, Ph.D., generously spent much of her vacation time reviewing the printed galley proofs. Her impressive ability to spot matters on the printed page that need attention must be related to having developed a keen eye in another language when she got her doctorate at Harvard in French literature years ago. Moreover, her extensive international sailing experience and her marriage to another sailor and former U.S. Navy officer, "Captain" John H. Watts, III, furthered her ability to cast a critical and constructive eye on this story about the sea.

History, it is said, is an account of events as told by the victor. However, in the video documentary and in this book I have tried to be factual, objective and fair-minded. Any shortcomings in this regard or mistakes or errors in the telling are mine.

Charles Raskob Robinson
December 24, 2014
(The bicentennial of the signing of the Treaty of Ghent)

Printed in Great Britain
by Amazon

81745728R00098